M5

B1ag

SCENES FROM
A CLERICAL LIFE

A stranger here
Strange things doth meet, strange glories see;
Strange treasures lodged in this fair world appear,
Strange all and new to me;
But that they mine should be, who nothing was,
That strangest is of all, yet brought to pass.

THOMAS TRAHERNE

SCENES FROM
A CLERICAL LIFE

AN AUTOBIOGRAPHY

———

ALEC R. VIDLER

Illustrations by
GEORGE MURRAY

COLLINS
ST JAMES'S PLACE, LONDON
1977

For
John Malcolm, Charles Patrick,
Peter Paul and Matthew Christian
Muggeridge

William Collins Sons & Co. Ltd
London · Glasgow · Sydney · Auckland
Toronto · Johannesburg

First published 1977
© Alec R. Vidler 1977
ISBN 0 00 216809 10
Set in Monotype Plantin
Made and printed in Great Britain by
William Collins Sons & Co. Ltd, Glasgow

Contents

——

Illustrations

CHAPTER I

A Sussex Childhood

The seventeenth-century historian, Thomas Fuller, who is one of my favourite authors, said of his birthplace, Aldwinkle in Northamptonshire: 'God in his providence fixed my nativity in a remarkable place.' I can say the same with even more justification. For Rye in East Sussex is one of the most beautiful, interesting, and indeed enchanting, towns in England. G. K. Chesterton compared it, I believe, with Siena and Assisi. It was a high standard of comparison, but Rye is in that class, though it cannot boast of having produced a famous saint.

As regards its social character at the time of my nativity, we may take the testimony of Henry James who had recently settled at Lamb House (which is a stone's throw from my home) and who soon after his arrival spoke of 'the special note of Rye, the feeling of the little hilltop community, bound together like a very modest, obscure and impecunious, but virtuous and amiable family.' And although by 1908 he was beginning to lament that Rye was 'going to the dogs with increase of population, villas, horrible cheap suburbs, defacements, general ruinations,' his fears were much exaggerated. The old area of Rye, situated on its hill crowned by the parish church, has never lost its traditional structure, and has in some respects improved in appearance during the present century. The inroads of the motor car have been more damaging than anything else to its quietude and charm.

Not only was I born in a remarkable town but in a remarkable house, the oldest house in Rye, the only part surviving above ground of a thirteenth-century friary. Situated in Church

7

View of Rye from the South East

Square, which is very like a cathedral close minus the clergy, it has a view over the marshes to Rye Harbour and the sea, of which one can never tire. The friars, for whom this house was built in 1263, were known as the Sacci or Friars of the Sack, because of the sackcloth habits that they wore. It was a community that was an offshoot of the Franciscan Movement and its official name was 'The Friars Repentant of Jesus Christ'. They were first established in Provence in 1245, and first appeared in England at Cambridge in 1257. A peculiarity of the order was that it admitted women as well as men, and this circumstance may have led to its suppression in the fourteenth century. Since then the house, in which I was born and am living today, has been a private house. It came into the possession of my family in 1801.

Not only was I born in a remarkable place and in a remarkable house but, as it seems to me, at a remarkable time, namely on 27 December 1899. That is, during the last few days of the nineteenth century, since I prefer the opinion that a century

ends when its enumeration departs from the calendar. In any case I was securely born within the reign of Queen Victoria and am a Victorian at least to that extent and in fact in several other respects as well.

When reading biographies and autobiographies I confess that I often skip the opening pages that deal with ancestry and genealogy, so that in consistency I must try to be brief under this head. But I could claim that my parents were hardly less remarkable than the place and time of my birth. The Vidler family, which probably originated in Hampshire, had settled at Ticehurst in Sussex in the late seventeenth century. They appear to have done well as yeoman farmers. The Rye branch moved here towards the end of the eighteenth century and were soon taking a prominent part in the life of the borough. About 1820 my great-grandfather started a business as a general merchant and shipowner, which became both prosperous and extensive in its operations. He shipped coal from the north of England and timber from the Baltic; a regular packet boat service was run to London and emigrants were taken as far as New York. Inland branches of the business, which could be reached by river from Rye, were soon established.

By the time of my birth the firm was known as 'Vidler and Sons Limited', and my father was employed in it. He subsequently became its managing director. Before his marriage he had been to South Africa hoping to join the Cape Mounted Police but his faulty eyesight disqualified him. After the First World War, during which he was in the army, he became a member of the Rye Corporation and, like his father and grandfather, served as mayor. He also became the historian of Rye, the founder of its museum, and eventually was made an honorary freeman of the borough.

My mother, née Edith Hamilton Roper, was born at Hamilton in Canada, where her parents happened to be at the time. Her father, Edward Roper FRGS, was a great traveller, an artist, and an author of travel books and adventure stories. There are pictures by him in the National Galleries of Canada and Australia. My mother, who was an only child, had travelled much when she was young, and in England they often moved house. Like other Ropers, they claimed hopefully but doubtfully to be descended from Margaret Roper, Thomas More's daughter. My grandfather, who was of a restless and exploring disposition, lived from hand to mouth, earning what he could by his paintings and books and articles (for example in the *Boys' Own Paper*), but never striking gold, although he went gold-digging in Australia. My mother inherited his aptitude for the arts. I remember being asked whether one of her copies of a Turner painting was an original. Early in my life she took up bookbinding and leather work, and so contributed industriously to the family budget. Until the 1920s my parents were far from affluent. My mother was a good manager and exceedingly affectionate, but like her father she was somewhat irascible, whereas my father was of a placid temperament and not easily ruffled or excited.

10

As a child I naturally had no idea what a rare place Rye was. I took it for granted that during the summer months artists should be sitting around in our cobbled streets, painting the fascinating buildings and views that met their gaze from every angle. For several summers before the First World War we let our house in Rye and decamped to a primitive but delightful cottage on a farm at Icklesham, four miles away, and there I acquired a predilection for country life which has never left me. My father used to bicycle into Rye daily to his business, but he had many hobbies. He kept quite a large apiary in the cottage garden, and he was a diligent collector of *Hymenoptera aculeata* (wild bees), of flints, of coins, and of anything that bore on the history of Rye. In some, but not all, of these pursuits I learned to assist him and to follow his example. Our summers at Clover Cottage, Icklesham, served as our holidays. We did not go away otherwise, except until 1911 for Christmas to stay with an aunt of my mother's who had a large house and garden at Tulse Hill in south-east London. From there my sister and I were taken to see the sights of the metropolis. I vividly remember seeing a moving picture for the first time at Brixton. My surviving grandparents lived at St Leonards and Lewes respectively, and so were within easy reach, as were many other near relations.

We had a lot of friends in Rye and in the surrounding villages, and in those days there were more children around and about and fewer elderly and retired people. There were a good many artists and literary folk. My parents knew Henry James quite well and used to supply his table with honey. He once kissed me in my pram, and said, 'What an intelligent-looking baby!' As a boy I used to meet him and pay my respects as he wandered round the streets of Rye, pausing to observe closely one thing or another. After I retired and returned to Rye (in 1967) I became friends with his manservant, Burgess Noakes. (Indeed I gave the address at his funeral.) In conversation with him I discovered much more about Henry James's way of life than I, or I suppose my parents, knew at the time. I am not myself an addict of his novels, and wish I could remember his brother, William James, who was often at Lamb House during my childhood, and for whom I came later to have a high regard both as a writer and as a philosopher.

My mother taught me to read and write. For writing she used copy-books, a method which has fallen into disrepute, but in my case it was effective. I flatter myself that my handwriting is better than most people's. In September 1906 I went for a year to a small private school in Rye, known as Sussex House School, where the fees were 15s. a term! Then in September 1907 I became a boarder at Ascham, Eastbourne, which was one of the numerous preparatory schools there. It had been founded by the Rev. W. N. Willis who was married to a first cousin of my father's.

Several boys among my relatives went to Ascham. I am pretty sure that in my case the fees were reduced. After I had been there for about a year, Mr Willis took over St Vincent's, another preparatory school in Eastbourne, which had run down but had larger buildings and better grounds. So we all moved there and the school was known as Ascham St Vincent's until after the Second World War when it reverted to the name Ascham and became the junior school of Eastbourne College.

With one exception that I will mention directly, I have nothing but pleasant recollections of my schooldays at Eastbourne. I got on tolerably well both at work and at games. I liked the assistant masters. The headmaster, to whom we gave the disagreeable name of 'The Bug', I regarded with more awe than affection, but he was evidently very competent. Odd things stick in the memory. I remember that the senior boys felt themselves privileged, when invited to take breakfast at the high table with the Willis family, to be given the crusts which they cut off their pieces of toast! Dickens in *Bleak House* says that old Mr Turveydrop gave Peepy the crusts of his toasts to eat. In 1910 there were two general elections. In those days the results came in over a period of about ten days. A big chart was set up in the school on which the number of seats won by each party was recorded as the results came in. We took our politics from our fathers (women had not yet the vote) and only one boy out of about eighty professed to be a Liberal. I silently admired his courage, and when I met him again many years later told him so.

Now for the curious episode which I did not enjoy and which nearly led to my expulsion from the school. We slept in dormitories of varying size. The one I was in at the time was comparatively small, but the beds were separated by a partition that was capable of being scaled. One evening there was an engagement over the top of the partition in which we had a spitting match with one another. We were discovered and I must have been regarded as the ring-leader. Anyhow I was severely taken to task by the headmaster and sent home the next morning with a view to being expelled. Though it is unpleasant enough to recall that one engaged in a spitting match, I was bewildered by the misdemeanour's being treated so seriously. When I reached home I found that my parents were greatly grieved, and my father took me for a walk down the garden and told me not to be 'a little pig'. However, they successfully pleaded for my reinstatement and I was allowed to return to school but had to sleep henceforth in a small bedroom by myself, so that I should not exercise a corrupting influence. It was only after I had left Ascham that I came to the conclusion that what I had been charged with was not merely spitting but some form of gross indecency, though precisely what form I still have no idea. Whatever it was I was innocent of it.

Like a great many children at that period I never received any instruction or explanation from my parents, teachers, or anyone else, about what are known as 'the facts of life'. At the time of which I am speaking I was not only ignorant of them but not interested in them. Later I got to know them all right by reading. I doubt if I was seriously handicapped by not receiving the kind of sex education about which so much trouble is taken nowadays. I fancy I might have received an inferior kind of instruction from two American boys who spent a year at Ascham and were older and more sophisticated than the rest of us. I recall their taking me apart furtively on the playground and unsuccessfully attempting to impart to me information about sex and what not. They were unsuccessful, because of what I later came to look upon as a fault or weakness in myself, namely the habit of being ashamed to appear ignorant and so of pretending to know more than I did. It would seem that there are circumstances in which this fault or weakness can have beneficial results.

Whether or not I was culpably deprived of a sexual education, I am thankful to say that I did receive a religious education. My mother was a devout evangelical Christian. So far as I can make out, her parents had been Baptists, but she had been baptized and confirmed as an Anglican in her 'teens at St John's Episcopal Church, Princes Street, Edinburgh. My father as a young man had been a regular churchgoer with a lively interest in theology, but in my childhood he seemed to be detached from the Church, though later he resumed attendance. It was my mother who taught me to pray and to read the Bible, and my sister and I accompanied her to matins in Rye church on Sunday mornings. We found it boring, but were allowed to scribble in prayer-books during the sermon. In a diary which I kept for the first three weeks of 1908, I find this entry on 19 January: 'Went to Rye Chruch. Played Chruch game.' I take that to be an indication not that I was already headed for the clerical state, but that in those days we were not supposed to play ordinary games on Sunday but were free to play at church. I remember reading at home a large bible with some gruesome illustrations, and enjoying the Old Testament stories. Much later I formed the opinion that young children should be brought up on the Old Testament and introduced to the New Testament, which is a book for adults, in maturer years. But I fear that this is an impracticable prescription.

The religious education of my home was continued at Ascham, where there was a chapel in the school building. I do not think I found that boring, though the only detail about the services that I recall is that we were instructed to stand up whenever the Lord's Prayer occurred in the reading of the Lessons, a practice which is not common but is not unheard of elsewhere.

In July 1912 I was offered scholarships at two minor public schools in Kent – St Lawrence College, Ramsgate, and Sutton Valence School, and choice had to be made between them. The choice that was made was not based upon an assessment of the comparative educational status of the two schools. It so happened that both my parents, before ever they knew or had heard of one another, had acquired close associations with Sutton Valence, a beautifully situated village overlooking the Weald of Kent.

When my paternal grandmother had been left as a young widow in 1873 with three boys to educate, she had moved from Rye to The Old Parsonage at Sutton Valence and sent the boys, of whom my father was the youngest, as day-boys to the school, and the family had remained there until their schooling had been completed. Some time afterwards the Ropers, i.e. my maternal grandparents and my mother, had rented for several years a house (The Limes) in the centre of the village, and had made many friends in the neighbourhood, including some of the masters at the school. Thus in 1912 both my parents were disposed to welcome the opportunity of reforging their links with a place that had many happy memories for them.

That is why I went to Sutton Valence School, and got roots in Kent as well as in Sussex. In the course of my life I have lived and worked in about ten counties and have come to appreciate the distinct excellencies of each, but Sussex has been my first and last love, and I agree with Cardinal Newman who said that it had always seemed to him the best county in England. Since 1910 or thereabouts I have faithfully followed the fortunes of the Sussex County Cricket Club and of no other.

CHAPTER II

The First World War

Sutton Valence is one of the many grammar schools that were founded in the Tudor period, often under the auspices of the City livery companies. This one was founded in 1576 by William Lambe, a Clothworker, and the Worshipful Company of Clothworkers were its governors until 1910, when they transferred it to the United Westminster Schools. A program of expansion was then set in motion. Large new buildings were erected, including two new boarding houses. A new headmaster was appointed, the Rev. W. W. Holdgate, who had taken a first class degree in natural science at Cambridge, and who was thus well qualified to balance the traditional classical curriculum of the school by the introduction of a science side.

When I went to the school in September 1912 the new regime was just getting into its stride or getting off the ground, as we say now. At the end of my diary for 1912 I wrote: 'Went to Sutton Valence school on 19 Sept. Liked it very much.' That continued to be the case. It has been my good fortune during most of my life to live in beautiful places, and the situation of Sutton Valence could hardly be bettered. There was a marvellous view from the school extending as far as Fairlight on the Sussex coast, and the village and its surroundings were worthy of the reputed garden of England. I seem to have got on well enough since my school reports that have survived show that I was usually at the top of my form. I was on the classical side of the school: I must be one of the last pupils in any school who never had a single lesson in the natural sciences. This has not, however, led to my being ignorant or unappreciative of scientific methods of study which have their place and importance in the arts as well as in the sciences, narrowly so-called.

My classics master, H. W. Hunting, was a splendid old-style public school master. He had joined the staff in 1885 when my father was still a boy at the school; he had got to know my mother when the Ropers were living in Sutton Valence in the early 1890s; and he did not retire till 1920. He was an excellent scholar and an able teacher, and I owe much to him. I have a letter that he wrote to my mother on 27 September 1914 that reminds me of things of which I have only a vague memory.

Just a line to tell you how pleased I am to have yr boy as House Prefect. He and his colleague – also a very good chap – take their duties most seriously & perform them most conscientiously. It wd have done your heart good to see, as I did last week, your boy patrolling the Dormitory *cane in hand* ready to drop on to any uproarious small boy. I am delighted with them both & they have eased my work very considerably.

It was a house for younger boys. I do appear to have been something of a disciplinarian, for towards the end of my school career when I was in the headmaster's house he wrote in my report for the Christmas term 1917: 'Has done very well as Head of the house & school. I am pleased with the state of discipline he has maintained in the house.'

But a variety of things had happened before then of which I have a clearer memory. Along with other boys I was confirmed in November 1914, having been well prepared by the headmaster who acted as chaplain of the school. There was not then a school chapel as there is now; the parish church was used for our Sunday services, and morning prayers on weekdays were in the school hall. I took confirmation seriously, and it was about that time that I came under the influence of a boy older than myself, named Ormiston (his nickname was Beaky, because of the prominence of his nose). He was to become a dedicated and devoted Roman Catholic priest, but he was now an ardent young Anglo-Catholic, who came from a parish in St Margaret's-on-Thames where that form of religion was strongly entrenched. The Anglo-Catholic movement in the Church of England was then in the ascendant and continued to be so till the 1930s.

It was through Ormiston that I was attracted to it together with another friend of mine, in fact my co-prefect in Mr Hunting's house. I fear that we became what in ecclesiastical jargon is known as a trio of spikes. Under Ormiston's guidance, who was in constant communication with his parish priest at home, we took to displaying our religious zeal outwardly by such actions as making the sign of the cross during school prayers and generally 'bowing and scraping', though what precisely is signified by 'scraping' in that Trollopian expression I am not sure.

Anyhow, our ostentatious behaviour naturally caused unfavourable comment in the school, and the headmaster very reasonably and temperately asked us to modify it, and I hope that we did so. There are, I suppose, worse things that schoolboys can get taken up with, but I do not recall this phase of my religious development with satisfaction. I am about to explain how I was away from school for a year in 1915–16. When I returned both my companions in the display of religiosity had left to join the army, and I myself had either lost my nerve or learned sobriety, so that there was no more trouble about this. Nevertheless, as will appear, it was by no means the end of my involvement with Anglo-Catholicism.

The First World War had broken out in August 1914. Its initial effects on the school were not considerable, except that the Officers Training Corps (OTC) assumed a new importance. The headmaster became its commanding officer, and he took his duties in that capacity with the same enthusiasm as he did his other pursuits. He was a keen astronomer and field naturalist. The effects of the war upon myself were more interruptive.

My father, who had once been a sergeant in the Cinque Ports Rifle Volunteers (whose history he was later to write) and then a trooper in the Sussex Imperial Yeomanry, was now in his middle forties, but he determined to apply for a commission in the army, and he became an officer in a regiment that was charged with home defence in various parts of south-east England and East Anglia. Between 1914 and 1917, when he was invalided out, he was stationed at Folkestone, Saltwood, Woolwich Arsenal, Canvey Island, Clacton-on-Sea and other places, at some of which my mother joined him. To begin with, he was only a lieutenant, and by the middle of 1915 it was evident that his pay was insufficient for the needs of his family. At the same time, it had not proved possible to remedy the shortage of staff that his absence had caused in the family business. Therefore, in order to kill two birds with one stone, it was decided that I should be withdrawn from school, at least for the time being, and be employed in the office of Vidler and Sons, Ltd.

I started work there immediately after the summer term, and seem quickly to have become well-suited to the business. The secretary of the firm, who was now in charge, was an admirable man of whom I became very fond. In the course of time he entrusted me with increasing responsibilities. At first, I dealt with correspondence, making out accounts, and keeping the books. I got to know well the employees of the firm, the bargees, and the skippers and mates of our sea-going ships. Later I used to visit by bicycle the branches of the business up country and check the accounts there. Altogether I became much attached to the work and to the persons engaged in it and would quite happily have made my career in the business. I am still glad to have had the experience, for at least it taught me some abidingly useful business-like habits.

Meanwhile, I was living at home and my leisure was fully occupied. I became a member of the Rye Volunteer Training Corps, which corresponded more or less to the Home Guard of the Second World War. Of the forty or so members of our detachment most were men over military age. We used to parade for drills, dig trenches, fill sandbags, and so on. Then, I became a server in the church at Rye and sang in the choir. There were many friends and relatives in and around Rye to visit, and there was sea-bathing in the summer. I also did a modicum, but only a modicum, of study.

By this time I was aware of a pull towards offering myself sooner or later for holy orders. I do not know just how or when this awareness originated. It certainly was not due to pressure or even suggestion from anyone else. My mother was sympathetic but not particularly encouraging to the idea, probably because she did not at all like my High Church proclivities. My father, while not unsympathetic, urged that it would be better to qualify for, and practise, some other profession, such as chartered accountancy, before taking so serious a step. He had a cousin who had followed that course. I thought that, if I was to be ordained, I should need a university degree, and during this year when I was at home I made some inquiries about the possibility of working for an external degree. I was presuming that in the meantime I should go on working in the family business and I was perfectly content to do so.

What changed my plans was the intervention of a generous friend of my mother's, Mrs Brady, who lived at Twickenham, but also had a house at Winchelsea, which enabled us often to meet. She had apparently formed the opinion that I was deserving of more education. My diary for 30 June 1916 says: 'cycled over to Winchelsea in the evening to see Mrs Brady about her offer to send me back to school by paying expenses.' My father unexpectedly arrived home later that evening and stayed the night, and despite a good deal of reluctance on my part it was agreed that this exceedingly benevolent proposal should be gratefully accepted. At the same time a married lady appeared on the scene who was well able to take my place. (She is still living, aged over a hundred, as a near neighbour of mine in Rye.)

So I returned to Sutton Valence on 22 September 1916. I had already received a note from the headmaster to say that I should be made a school prefect, and a year later I was made head of the school, both of which promotions seem to me more surprising now than perhaps they did at the time. The impact of the war on the life of the school was much more noticeable than it had been before. Our games were sometimes interrupted by the passage of zeppelins overhead. My diary records that aeroplanes came down in the neighbourhood of the school on a number of occasions. I was secretary of a war savings association that was started. I suppose that we must have complained about food rationing, but I do not remember doing so. I am sure that I had no reason to do so during two school holidays during which I worked on farms, in one case helping with the harvest near Bury St Edmunds, and in the other trapping rabbits, moles and rats near Didcot in Berkshire.

What I found most disagreeable was that four afternoons a week were given over to the OTC. This was not calculated to instil ardour for a military career. But boys older than myself were at intervals being called up, and I took it for granted that like the rest I should in due course depart to the wars. Once conscription had been introduced we did not have to face the question of volunteering. It did not occur to any of us to be pacifists.

Masters naturally were called up too, if they had not already volunteered, and were replaced by some rather odd substitutes. One of them, a keen scouter, turned out to be a pederast and had to go. Another, Groom by name, but nicknamed Pimpo, I got to like. He started a discussion group which met to read papers on literary and political topics. I read a paper on Disraeli whose novels I was then reading. During my last term, there was the innovation of a woman on the teaching staff. The only thing I recall about her, apart from her name and her indifferent looks, is that she wore a mortar board with a large hole cut out of the back of it to make room for her bun. This may have been a usual feminine fashion, but I had not struck it before.

I took an active part in the school debating society and I have a record of some of the motions that I either proposed or supported, but I cannot be sure that they expressed my real opinions since I may already have learned that a good debater is prepared to speak to any motion whether he believes it or not, and that in conversation we are not on oath. But, for what they are worth, here are one or two propositions that I supported: 'that the development of the Labour Movement threatens danger to the State'; 'that England has seen her best days'; and 'that the principles of socialism should be adopted in England'.

My diary reminds me that in March 1918 there was a strange episode which as head of the school I had to handle and which looks like an early assertion of pupil, or at least of prefectorial, power. During some OTC manoeuvres one of the school prefects took part in a charge with naked bayonet fixed, presumably by an oversight on his part; in any case no injury took place. The headmaster was as usual the officer commanding. He was a quick-tempered man and he flogged the culprit there and then in the open. We prefects regarded this not only as a wrong kind of punishment but as an insult to a prefect and therefore to all of us. We met and decided that we would all resign if the injustice were not repaired. When I went to see the headmaster with two other prefects (one of whom was his son!), he acknowledged that he had acted hastily and had forgotten for the moment that the boy he had flogged was a prefect, and (my diary adds) 'he knuckled under entirely to all our points'.

The incident leads me to recall a fact which in retrospect I find shocking, namely that we boys at school were taught how to kill Germans by plunging a naked bayonet into stuffed sacks suspended in a row from a bar, like the cross bar of a football goal. However desirable or necessary pre-military training may have been deemed to be, this exercise now seems to me to have been intolerable. If we had to learn and practise it, it would have been time enough when we were actually in the army – which I was soon to be.

I expected to be called up during the summer of 1918, but I hoped to be allowed to complete the summer term at school. I had already without success taken the scholarship examinations at St John's College, Cambridge, and Pembroke College, Oxford. Any chance I might have had of winning a classical scholarship had, I apprehend, been substantially lessened by my year away from school. I received my calling-up papers on 28 June and reported at the National Service Area Headquarters at Brighton on 1 July.

On the day I left Sutton Valence I made the following entry in my diary which betrays or conceals a degree of emotion that hardly ever finds expression there: 'My feelings of loss and regret at departure and untimely conclusion of this my school career are too manifold, almost too sacred, to be recorded or summed up in verbal phrases.' This entry is consistent with the 'portentous solemnity' which some of my elders, I dare say correctly, alleged to be one of my characteristics. Thus Mr Hunting wrote to my mother on 15 October 1917:

> I have been trying ever since the beginning of term to write a line telling you how extremely glad I was to find Alex at last Head of the School – a position he thoroughly deserves . . . I liked him from the very first, & I think he likes me a little, but he is so completely self-contained that it is difficult to judge. Indeed the only fault I ever found in him was that he is so portentously solemn.

My military career was short – of exactly six months' duration – and can be recorded briefly. In the First World War, if you were in a school OTC, you were not called up to serve in the ranks, but sent straight to a unit where you were trained to become a commissioned officer. I went into the Royal

Field Artillery and spent my first six weeks at the Preston barracks, Brighton, where we were sorted out and received some preliminary instruction, before being sent on to an Officers Cadet School. At Brighton we slept on boards and palliasses, and I remember reading in bed a paperback edition of *John Inglesant*. I spent a week or two in the sick bay, suffering from influenza and the effects of inoculation. When I was allowed to go out, I was attired in the blue uniform with a red tie that wounded soldiers wore, and I found that I was admitted free of charge to the Brighton cinemas.

In the middle of August I was sent to the Officers Cadet School at Weedon in Northamptonshire, which was pleasantly situated. Some of us were, like me, straight from school, but most were NCOs back from France who were now training to return there as officers. Much of our time was spent with horses, riding, driving gun carriages, and looking after them by day and night. All this I thoroughly enjoyed. We also had to do a lot of theoretical and practical work with guns which I found less agreeable. I am astonished to find that in one of my letters home I reported that I was one of the few cadets to have been complimented on my showing in an examination in gunnery.

My letters home, which my parents preserved, were frequent but commonplace, mostly about food, day-to-day details, and disappointed expectations of leave with occasional and cheerful comments on the war news, such as: 'The news is ever so good; our chances of seeing any of the sport seem to be diminishing daily' (10 October 1918). To my grandmother I had written in September: 'Things certainly are looking brighter than anyone could ever have anticipated, but I hope it won't be quite all over before I get out even if it is only a case of marching into Berlin.' I had not myself expected so early an end to the war. A journal that I had begun to write in from time to time has this entry: 'When I joined up in July I quite thought the war would be on for three or four years more. I thought with para-

doxically mingled feelings of hope and dread that I should be
face to face with death in the trenches' (8 January 1919).

At Weedon we were more comfortably accommodated than
at Brighton and I had plenty of congenial companions. The only
one with whom I formed a permanent friendship was W. W.
Williamson (who always signed his letters W³). He must have
been in his thirties then. Neither by physique nor by general
aptitude was he cut out for military service, but he was excellent
company with conservative social and literary interests and an
admiration for Bishop Gore. He later became general manager of
the Norwich Union Insurance Society, and I visited him more
than once at Lamas Hall, near Norwich. I chance to remember
a remark of an ex-public schoolboy cadet, whose home was in
Half Moon Street, London. He told me that his father said
that you might agree or disagree with Bergson, but when you
had read him your thinking could never be the same again.
This implies that we had more interesting things to talk about
than shop or sex.

The armistice on 11 November opened up fresh prospects
for me as well as for others. Some time before, negotiations had
been completed for my admission to Selwyn College, Cambridge,
after the war. I was released from the army at the beginning of
January 1919, receiving my commission as a second lieutenant
only after I had been demobilized. I cannot say that I derived
much benefit from my short experience of military life, except
for horse riding, a pastime in which unfortunately I have seldom
been able to indulge since then.

CHAPTER III

Cambridge and Wells

Selwyn College, Cambridge, had been founded in 1882 in memory of George Augustus Selwyn who was one of the heroes of the Victorian Church. When I entered its portals on 14 January 1919 it still bore signs of its comparatively recent origin. The attractive sunken lawn in the court (since then lamentably filled in and levelled up) was disfigured by a temporary building that had at first served as a chapel and was now the library. For most practical purposes Selwyn had acquired the same status in the university as the older colleges, though it was technically still known as a 'public hostel', a limitation that irked the Master and fellows more than it did the undergraduates. Dr J. O. F. Murray was Master at the time.

Although not restricted to members of the Church of England, Selwyn was closely identified with the Church and under-graduates were required to attend more chapel services than in other colleges. There had always been a substantial proportion of candidates for ordination, but it was in no sense a theological college even if some people regarded it as such. One of the aims of the founders had been that it should provide for simple and inexpensive standards of living so as to enable less affluent parents to send their sons there. In those days state grants were not available in the way they are now. I presume that I was entered for Selwyn mainly for economic reasons. I did have a grant from a church fund, known as the Service Candidates Fund, which was designed to help ex-servicemen to be ordained. The college also awarded me an exhibition. While my bank balance was always extremely modest, I seem to have managed all right and never ran into debt. One did plenty of entertaining of one's friends, but it was nearly always for tea or coffee.

My tutor and supervisor of studies was S. C. Carpenter, who later became Master of the Temple and Dean of Exeter – an amiable man with a gracious style and liberal sympathies. It was on his advice that I read for the theological tripos, which in those days was a three-year course, embracing not only the Bible in Hebrew and Greek, but also the history and doctrine of the early Church. I have never regretted that I took his advice. Apart from its obvious utility to an intending priest, the study of theology, so far from being narrowing, is broadening to the mind. It involves languages and literature, the history of ideas and institutions, and philosophy, and branches out into a large variety of specialized disciplines. It seems strange, however, that when I took the tripos, we had to study no history after AD 461, which gave the subject a misleadingly archaeo-logical appearance. Whether or not for that reason, I sub-sequently became most interested in modern Church history. Anyone embarking on the study of theology at the university has to be rigorously initiated into the critical study of the Bible which some, then and now, have found to be disturbing to their faith as Christians. It may be due to Carpenter's skilful initiation that it did not have that effect on me. On the contrary, it quickly became of absorbing and rewarding interest, and what is known as 'radical' criticism has never had any terrors for me. Of course I had to set about thinking out the grounds or rationale of my faith in a way I had not had to do before, and there is bound to be stress and tension in doing that unless one closes one's mind to dangerous thoughts. I shall have more to say about this later.

I must confess that I was not much excited by the theologians whose lectures I attended, except for C. E. Raven, who was then Dean of Emmanuel College and whom I had long admired, since the Raven family used to spend their summer holidays at

Cambridge – The Backs

Rye and Charles would often be invited to preach. I think I learned most of what I did learn as an undergraduate through reading and discussion with my friends. But I may be doing an injustice to my formal instructors. I did most of my reading during the vacations, and in term time engaged in the extra-curricular pursuits of a normal undergraduate. I joined the Union and the University Musical Society (CUMS), the conductor of which was the formidable Dr Rootham of St John's College. I appear to have shed my 'portentous solemnity'. My diary records that I was implicated on one 'November the fifth' in organizing an abortive raid by Selwyn men on Newnham College which is next door to Selwyn. I recall with shame that on another occasion I was instrumental in putting a hedgehog in the bed of a refractory fellow-undergraduate. I also founded one of those ephemeral college societies that have

a tie and not much else to them. Ours called itself 'the Man-drakes'.

During the war the university had been almost denuded of undergraduates and many dons had naturally been away on war work. It is remarkable how quickly in January 1919 the life of the university and colleges began to revive. Some men who had been up before the war came back into residence but most of us were freshmen, ex-army or straight from school. Selwyn from its earliest days had become renowned for its prowess of the river. For a new and small college it had produced an impressive run of proficient oarsmen, and as races between the colleges were to be resumed in my first term (though on this occasion they were to be not bumping races, but timed) the pre-war rowing men were eager to get a boat on the river at once. One of my first Selwyn friends, A. H. Brown, who was also reading theology, had rowed at school and so was an obvious recruit, and he succeeded in carrying me along with him. Rugby football and cricket were the games for which I had so far had a penchant and a certain aptitude and I had had no intention of rowing, but I was unable to resist the appeal to show loyalty to the college at a moment when numbers were few and talent scarce.

I cannot say that I ever enjoyed it much, but we had some success in the Lent and May races 1919, and I was actually awarded my first Lent and May colours. My diary mentions that in the first race in which I took part (26 February 1919) Selwyn beat King's by one second! In the following year (1919–20) I tried to get out of rowing, partly because it took up too much time and because I wanted to play the games that I enjoyed. All I did on the river thereafter was some incompetent coaching, and I rowed in the May races 1920. I do not regret having rowed since it enabled me ever afterwards to take an intelligent interest in an accomplishment that arouses much enthusiasm in its adepts.

My most agreeable memories of university life are of the friendships that I made. I have already named A. H. Brown with whom I had much in common. He had been the head chorister of St Paul's Cathedral, and I frequently accompanied him to evensong in King's College chapel. His appreciation of the singing was much more expert than mine, but it enraptured me as it has done ever since. Brown shared my Anglo-Catholic dispositions, though he was more restrained in his expression of them. We both became members of the High Church society in the university known as STC (*Sacrae Trinitatis Confraternitas*), and in my third year I became secretary of it. We were both present at the first Anglo-Catholic Congress which was held in the Albert Hall in the summer of 1920, when one of the speakers was G. K. Chesterton, though he was almost inaudible in such a building. There was a very large attendance and great missionary enthusiasm. It probably marked the high-water mark of Anglo-Catholic aspirations to convert the Church of England, and indeed the people of England, to the kind of doctrine and the style of worship and devotion by which the movement was animated.

I myself with another Selwyn friend (G. A. B. Newenham) had the memorable experience of staying during the congress in the same house (The House of Charity in Greek Street, Soho) as Frank Weston, Bishop of Zanzibar. During my undergraduate years Frank Weston moved and inspired me when he visited Cambridge more than any other speaker. He was a wonderful Christian despite his reputation as a controversialist and his attacks on the higher critics which always jarred on my mind. I remember Charles Raven's saying during a lecture that Weston's book *The One Christ* was the most important contribution to the study of christology that had so far appeared in the twentieth century. Other visitors to Cambridge who particularly impressed me were Handley Moule, Bishop of Durham, and the Sadhu Sundar Singh, a saintly Indian Christian mystic, who stayed in the Master's Lodge at Selwyn for a day or two in March 1920. About the same time there was a mission to the university conducted by Charles Gore and others during which I made my first confession, a painful but salutary practice that I have maintained ever since.

Another early and close friend of mine at Selwyn was Philip Strong, who was to have a distinguished career as Bishop of New Guinea during the Second World War, as Archbishop of Brisbane, and finally as Primate of the Anglican Church in Australia. He was, and is, a man of ardent, unclouded and infectious faith. I admired and envied his apostolic zeal. He influenced me a lot and we have maintained an affectionate contact ever since.

Nowadays all Cambridge colleges have an official nurse and other medical facilities for their members. It was not so then. Undergraduates were dependent on their friends unless their ailments were serious enough for them to go into a hospital or nursing home. I remember acting as nurse to Philip Strong during a quite severe attack of shingles that afflicted him, and we used to wonder whether the rash, or whatever it should be called, was going to meet round his middle, which we understood would be fatal. Fortunately, it didn't. Just at the same time Brown was attacked by diptheria, a common and serious illness in those days, but he was removed to an isolation hospital where his friends visited him so far as they were permitted to do so.

In September 1920, Brown, Strong and I took part in the Cambridge University Missionary Campaign in the Potteries, in which Stephen Neill was a moving spirit. Between fifty and a hundred undergraduates stayed there for ten days and preached in churches and spoke in schools, and other places, in the cause of overseas missions. I do not know that our endeavours had much effect on our auditories, but it was a useful experience for us. It was my first excursion into the world of heavy industry and among other things we were taken down a coal mine.

The closest and most enduring friendship that I made at Selwyn was with Malcolm Muggeridge. I need not say anything about his subsequent career since it is sufficiently well known. He came up in my third year, i.e. in October 1920. So far as I can tell from my diary I did not get to know him till the Lent term 1921 and then in circumstances that hardly augured well. I had rashly undertaken to coach the Selwyn 3rd Lent boat and both Malcolm and Philip Strong were to row in it. Neither the coach nor the oarsmen and still less the cox (a man with the curious name of Grandorge) were well qualified for their respective tasks. In the Lent races the boat fared disastrously, going down four places, and on none of the four days reaching First Post Corner (Cambridge rowing men will understand how humiliating this was). On the first day Philip Strong caught a crab. On the second day the boat never really got under weigh: 'catastrophic loss of rudder line by cox at start', my diary says!

However, despite these unpropitious circumstances, Malcolm and I quickly became attached to one another. I admit that I am surprised to discover that in the following term we constantly played tennis together, even entering as partners for a doubles tournament. I say 'surprised' because our relationship was never afterwards based on sporting affinities! He was three or four years younger than I and had quite a different background, but already, I should say, he had that charm of personality that has won him a host of friends among those who have met him in real life as distinguished from people who have encountered him only through the media. I think that I also detected in those early days that potentially he had a kind of genius as a talker and writer and even as a seer. That this was so was not indicated by his academic record. It was a grave mistake that he was put to study natural science instead of an arts subject.

Anyhow, we became, and continued to be, fast friends through all the changes and chances of our different lives. When I first got to know him he was being prepared for confirmation by S. C. Carpenter who was his tutor as well as mine, and I was present at his confirmation in Queens' College chapel on 6 March 1921. I do not consider that in his autobiography he has adequately assessed the sincerity and depth of his initiation into Christian faith and practice at this time, though doubtless, as in all of us, they were compounded with other interests and inclinations. If for my part I was naturally eager to support and encourage him in the Christian way, he influenced me more obviously and decisively, partly through introducing me to his father.

We visited each other's homes during the summer vacation of 1921. It must have been one day when he was staying at my home that Malcolm and I took a walk along the beach at Rye Harbour and as the tide was high, the weather warm and no one else seemed to be about, we stripped and entered the sea. No sooner had we done so than there appeared from nowhere

Mrs C. (a lady whom my mother had pointed out to me some years before as the first woman in Rye to wear a hobble skirt) and her daughter Lena. They settled down on the beach opposite to where we were swimming. I suppose in these brazen days we should have emerged from the water *in puris naturalibus* and have chatted them up. But modesty kept us swimming around much longer than we had intended, as our spectators proved very reluctant to move away.

When I visited the Muggeridges at Croydon I at once fell under the spell of Malcolm's father who was soon to become a Labour MP. He was one of those devoted idealists with a passionate desire to win justice for the poor and underprivileged, who then abounded in the Labour Party. He had already visited Cambridge in the May term, and I had written in my diary: 'Mr Muggeridge I fell in love with right away – in fact I think I had done so long before I ever saw him,' i.e. from what Malcolm had told me about him. I was already, maybe, a theoretical socialist of sorts, since at the end of my 1920 diary I wrote: 'My political sympathies tend to the Labour Party.' But it was Malcolm and his father who made a convert of me, with some practical results as will appear.

I may have been by temperament a bit of an agitator or reformer. The present Master of Selwyn has told me that in the college archives there is evidence that in 1920 I promoted an appeal against compulsory chapels, i.e. for making attendance voluntary. My diary also reminds me that I wrote to urge the Master that the inscription on the college war memorial should be in English, not Latin, because the names of college servants were to be included and their relatives could not be expected to understand Latin. The latter point now seems rather trivial but the former was important.

I sat for the tripos examination at the end of May 1921. I had scraped a first in the preliminary examination in the previous year but had hardly expected to do so well in the tripos and so was not unduly disappointed when I got a II.1. I had no

Wells

academic ambitions. My only aim was to be either a missionary overseas or a priest in a slum parish in England. As regards the former, various projects were afoot in which I was interested, one of which developed into the Christa Seva Sangha in India in which Algy Robertson, Verrier Elwin and Jack Winslow were the principal participants. As regards the latter, on 28 April 1921 I heard Father Harold Ellis (later a member of the Community of the Resurrection) speak in Cambridge about his

35

work at the Mission of the Holy Spirit in Newcastle-upon-Tyne, and he kindled my desire to work in the north of England and in a parish like that which he described. But the next thing I had to do was to spend a year and a half at a theological college.

I had applied for admission to Wells rather than to Ely or Cuddesdon which were the best-known Anglo-Catholic colleges for graduates. My mother, who had often stayed at Wells, had brought me up to conceive of it as one of the most beautiful places in England, as indeed it is. Then, I wanted to go to a college that was not identified with one party in the Church: already I must have been developing an antipathy to sectarianism. Another attraction of Wells was that associated with the college were a number of mission churches in the surrounding villages. Students were assigned to one of these and so gained some practical experience of parish and pastoral work. I went to Wells on 29 July 1921 and was assigned to the mission at Greenore on top of the Mendips. This was the aspect of my time at Wells that I most enjoyed. We went up to Greenore for a service on Sundays and spent Friday afternoons visiting our parishioners.

Wells was singular among theological colleges in that it had no recognizable building to which one could point as 'The College'. The students lived in lodgings in the charming old houses in the Vicars' Close, though in my time there was also a residential hostel known as 'The Cedars'. But I opted to live in the Vicars' Close, where I shared a largish house (No. 16) with two or three other men, one of whom A. M. Jones, then a hearty scouting enthusiast, became afterwards an authority on African music and taught it at the School of African and Oriental Studies in London University. The college used either the cathedral or the little chapel in the Vicars' Close for its services. There was an excellent library and, as I did not have to work for any examination and was expected to attend only a few lectures, I was free to read on my own and to go further into questions that had engaged my mind when I was working for the tripos. There was plenty of scope for games and I was elected captain of the rugby football team. I also took up hockey and recall the trepidation I felt when I had to keep goal in a match that we played against the boys of Downside School.

The most eminent theologian at Wells at this time was the Dean, Dr Armitage Robinson. We got to know him slightly, but did not see as much of him as we could have wished. He attended the cathedral infrequently. It was said that he had reached a level of piety which entitled him to sit lightly to public worship. (I was told later that his successor, Dr R. H. Malden, known as Pompey Malden, on the other hand, was a regular attender at the cathedral and, as is usual with deans, was always fetched from the deanery by a verger carrying a wand, which led an irreverent inhabitant of Wells to exclaim: 'Doesn't the old bugger know the way yet?'!)

The Archbishop of Canterbury (Davidson) was a friend of Armitage Robinson and stayed at the deanery for holy week and Easter. He gave a talk to the college about the present position of Anglicanism. In my journal I noted: 'He struck me as a very great, tactful, cautious statesman: a great pilot in these troublous times.' A few days later Dr W. E. Orchard, who was then well-known as a 'free Catholic' at the King's Weigh House in London, visited Wells and gave some of us a fascinating account of his ideas. Not long afterwards he became a Roman Catholic and ceased to be of interest. The Principal of the college, G. A. Hollis, was a holy man but distressingly shy; the Vice-Principal, H. B. Salmon (afterwards Principal) seemed to be more interested in sport than in theology; I specially liked the Chaplain, A. H. Cullen, who became bishop of Grahamstown; and, not least, I esteemed Prebendary H. P. Denison (nephew of the famous reactionary Archdeacon G. A. Denison) who had retired to Wells and represented the highest pitch of Anglo-Catholicism.

Nevertheless, I was soon disenchanted with Wells. I do not

think that I had by then read Trollope, but if I had I should have looked upon Wells as a contemporary manifestation of Barchester. It exuded the odour of establishment in every sense of that word. It stood for moderation and caution and the virtues associated with public schools. With a few exceptions the students in the college appeared to love to have it so, while I was in revolt against all that. Within a month of our coming to Wells another student and I ran into Eric Milner-White whom we had known at Cambridge as Dean of King's and a member of the Oratory of the Good Shepherd. (I realize now that he will have been running his annual camp for choristers in the neighbourhood of Wells.) He came to lunch with us and we told him about our discontents. He advised that if we found Wells intolerable we should transfer to Ely. In the event I stayed at Wells for a year but succeeded in negotiating that I should then leave and spend my last six months before ordination at the Oratory House, Cambridge.

I shall have more to say later about the Oratory House and the Oratory of the Good Shepherd, which is a community of celibates that had been founded in Cambridge in 1912 and had been increasing in membership there and elsewhere. After the war, its superior, John How, had given up his chaplaincy at Trinity College in order to open the Oratory House in Lady Margaret Road as a home for the community (some of whose members were working in colleges in the university), as a house of studies, and as a centre for pastoral work among undergraduates. I had been introduced to John How by Philip Strong. Other members of the community frequented the house even if they did not live there. I was especially fond of Wilfred Knox who was normally in residence, though he was liable to disappear into the east end of London to help some harassed priest there.

In September 1922 I attended the annual retreat of the Oratory, and already in the previous December, my diary reminds me, I had been considering the possibility of sooner or later

38

asking to become a member. The six months which I now spent in the house strengthened this hope. Other residents were Dr Joseph Needham who used to carry out scientific experiments in his bed-sitting-room, and Dr Frederick Brittain who acted both as cellarer and as cantor. Wilfred Knox was tone-deaf, but his theological stance, as well as his kind of spirituality and his sparkling humour, greatly appealed to me. His book *The Catholic Movement in the Church of England* was about to be published. He gave me a bit of research to do in connection with the work about St Paul on which he was engaged.

Malcolm Muggeridge was of course still at Selwyn and I was able to see a great deal of him during these six months, thus cementing our friendship. He often came to the Oratory House and later on resided there as he has recorded in his memoirs.

I had heard in May 1922 that there was likely to be a vacancy for an assistant priest at the Mission of the Holy Spirit in Newcastle, which seemed almost too good to be true. I had visited Father Ellis's successor there in June. By the end of July I had been definitely invited to serve my title there, as the saying is. The Bishop of Newcastle (Dr H. L. Wild) agreed to ordain me deacon on 28 December, since I would not have attained the statutory age for ordination when he held his regular ordination service in Advent.

Thus I was ordained in his private chapel at Benwell. My mother and sister were present (they stayed with cousins of ours at Sunderland), and Philip Strong (who had just been ordained in the neighbouring diocese of Durham to serve as curate of St Mary's, Tyne Dock), and a group of people from the Mission of the Holy Spirit. 'Wonderful – beyond words,' I wrote in my journal. I remember that Philip remarked on an amusing mistake that was made by the bishop. In the form of service which was designed for the ordination of several deacons, the bishop puts the question: 'Will you apply all your diligence to frame and fashion your own lives, and the lives of your families, according to the doctrine of Christ?' In putting the question to me, he said: 'your own life, and the lives of your families,' implying that I had a variety of natural children! Since I was ordained immediately after my twenty-third birthday, there was probably a month or so when I was the youngest clergyman in the Anglican Communion.

CHAPTER IV

Tyneside and English Catholicism

The Mission of the Holy Spirit served the lower and more
disreputable half of the large parish of St Philip's in the High
Elswick area of the city. The mission building, which was on
top of a coal mine, comprised a well-furnished church in the
semi-basement, a church hall and offices above, and a residence
in the two top stories where the Priest-in-Charge, his assistant
and a housekeeper lived. It was situated in a street that was most
incongruously called 'Spring Garden Lane'. The name derived
from the fact that, in the eighteenth century before Newcastle
expanded, this was the location of 'Spring Gardens' where
weekly concerts were held; they were described as 'a fair grass
field, ornamented with trees, used as a place of genteel resort,
where the gay and fashionable are entertained in tents with
music, singing, etc.' The district, as I knew it, flatly con-
tradicted that description in practically every respect.

It was by general consent one of the very worst slums on
Tyneside. It was on the slopes of a long hill above St James'
Park where Newcastle United play football (I could see into a
corner of the ground from my study window). There was row
after row of squalid houses with nothing to relieve their mono-
tony except the public houses, of which there had originally
been twenty-two in the parish together with twelve off-licence
beer shops in case the distances between the pubs were too
great for diligent drinkers. The number may have been
reduced a little by the 1920s. In the mission district the houses
were for the most part occupied by two, three or four families,
who often had little more than one room each.

Newcastle-upon-Tyne

The only commodity that appeared to be in good supply was coal which was the sole available means of cooking and heating, though in the clergy house we did have gas fires. Smoke emerged from chimneys all day long and the atmosphere was so smoke-laden that whenever you went out you returned with a coating

of dirt. Most people did not have their chimneys swept, but set them on fire periodically in order to clean them out. As our residence soared well above the surrounding dwellings, we received the full force of this obnoxiously smelly, dangerous and illegal operation. During an afternoon's visiting I often discovered that I had picked up a collection of fleas. Then, I remember dear Mrs T., a devout communicant, who lived in one room with thirteen cats; when she approached the altar, I can tell you that there was (what the Revised Standard Version of the Bible at John 11:39 delicately calls) an odour.

Shocking as were the housing conditions, I found the people who lived in and around Spring Garden Lane uniformly friendly and lovable. In fact I rapidly lost my heart to Tyneside and have had a painful nostalgia for it ever since. At first I had much difficulty in understanding the dialect. I notice that at the end of my engagement book for 1923 I made a glossary of twenty or thirty words that I had not come across before but were in everyday use in the parish. But I soon mastered the lingo and enjoyed talking it, especially with the children, many of whom had no shoes or stockings and were dressed in rags.

While I found our parishioners delightful, I cannot pretend that they were always on their best behaviour. There was much rowdiness and drunkenness, and the police either went about in pairs or kept out of the way. When there was a street fight at night, I used to get up, don my cassock and biretta, and go out to separate the combatants who might be women tearing at each other's hair. Mercifully they had a superstitious regard for a priest, provided he was properly attired, and would do for us what they would not have done for the police.

The founder and first Priest-in-Charge of the Mission of the Holy Spirit had been Vibert Jackson, an ideal missioner for such a district, flamboyant and aggressive and inspiring much affection in those whose cause he espoused. He left a legendary name behind him. He later became Bishop of the Windward Islands and lived to a great age. The Bishop of Newcastle in his time (Straton by name) was an extreme Low Churchman and did not at all approve of the goings-on at the mission which, I believe, he placed under a ban. But he was no match for Vibert Jackson.

When I went to Newcastle, Harold Ellis, whom I have

44

previously mentioned, had ceased to be in charge of the mission and had been succeeded by Ronald Wainwright, an exemplary priest who had been on the staff of St Matthews', Westminster, and who had been educated at Rugby and Trinity College, Cambridge. I am immensely indebted to him for the training he gave me in the various elements of priestcraft, which is a word that should not be used pejoratively. I must now say something about the religion that the mission existed to propagate and about my own beliefs at this period.

As I have said before, the Anglo-Catholic Movement probably reached its high-water mark in the early 1920s. It was a development of the Oxford or Tractarian Movement of the 1830s. That, in its first phase, had been mainly academic, concerned with rediscovering a high doctrine of the Church as a community distinct from, and with higher claims upon man's allegiance than, the State. It also emphasized the importance of the sacraments and stood for austere standards of moral and spiritual discipline. After the 1840s it lost its hold on the academic world and moved out into the parishes, not least into the slum parishes which then abounded in all large cities. Here it took to expressing itself in colourful and dramatic forms of worship, and it tended more or less to adopt, or rather to adapt, the *cultus* and pastoral methods of contemporary Roman Catholicism. The Anglo-Catholic clergy became known as 'ritualists' and throve on the opposition that they met with from ecclesiastical authority and from English Protestantism with its horror of what it called 'popery'. By the early twentieth century the movement had become more respectable and was exerting a considerable influence throughout the Anglican communion. The First World War gave it something of a boost. The Mission of the Holy Spirit was regarded as one of its advanced outposts in the north of England, and I was happy to be identified with it.

However, it was during the 1920s that various rifts became

apparent in the movement that prevented it from going on from strength to strength. It was the period when the long drawn out process of producing a revision of the Book of Common Prayer was coming to a head, and there were deeply felt differences of opinion among the Anglo-Catholics, as indeed among other groups in the Church of England, about the kind of revision that was needed. There had been a growing divergence between those, on the one hand, who favoured a style of worship that looked back to the Middle Ages in England (often called 'the English Use') and those, on the other hand, who wanted to assimilate Anglican worship as far as possible to that of contemporary western, that is, Roman, Catholicism, though only very few went so far as to want to introduce the Latin liturgy. The Mission of the Holy Spirit, and I myself, influenced by Wilfred Knox who was my principal mentor at this time, favoured the latter course, though there was no question of our going Latin.

Undoubtedly anyone visiting our mission church might easily have mistaken it for a Roman Catholic conventicle: my mother was deeply distressed when she first saw it. We insisted, so far as we could, on a standard of practice like that of the Roman Catholics, for example, attendance at mass on Sundays and holidays of obligation, auricular confession, fasting communion, and so on. Our principal morning service at the mission was a sung family mass at 9.30 a.m. which was much less common then than it is now, and on saints' days there was a sung mass at 6.30 a.m. to which quite a good congregation came. And of course there were one or more early masses every day. It was a kind of religion that seems to me to have had more substance to it, and to have been more wholesomely demanding, than what is prevalent now, even in reputedly Catholic circles.

Another difference within the Anglo-Catholic Movement was of a more recondite character and did not directly affect our evangelistic and pastoral work. It was a difference of theological orientation, which had first attracted attention when a volume of essays entitled *Lux Mundi* had been published in 1889. That had signalized the fact that a new generation of Oxford theologians, headed by Charles Gore, was not prepared to maintain the extremely conservative and backward-looking posture of the original tractarians, but was determined to come to terms with the new knowledge about the nature of the world and the history of mankind that had been making its way among educated people during the nineteenth century. In particular, they recognized the need to appropriate the fruits of the critical study of the Bible. Those who went along with *Lux Mundi* came to be known as 'liberal Catholics' in contrast to the old guard of whom the aforementioned Archdeacon G. A. Denison had been a stalwart representative.

The term 'liberal Catholic' had already been applied to several groups of Roman Catholics in England and on the Continent with varying connotations. My own sympathies, then and later, were especially with a group of liberal Roman Catholics, known as 'the Catholic Modernists', who struck me as, in the best sense, both more catholic and more liberal than their more cautious, moderate and dull Anglican counterparts. They had been ruthlessly suppressed by the papacy, but Anglicans were at liberty to acclimatize their ideas. The Anglo-Catholic clergy as a whole were not (in my opinion) intellectually adventurous or enterprising and tended to be fearful of any form of modernism, or at best were not inclined to move their inherited landmarks any further than the much respected, but fundamentally traditionalist, Bishop Gore had been willing to do.

The issues were raised in the 1920s by a group of predominantly Cambridge theologians who produced a volume of essays with the significant title, *Essays Catholic and Critical*. Some of the essayists were more critical than others: I specially appreciated the contributions of Wilfred Knox, A. E. J. Rawlinson and Will Spens. I shall return to this subject in the next chapter but one.

It happens that I have preserved the scripts of a course of four sermons that I preached in 1924 on 'English Catholicism' (a title that I preferred to 'Anglo-Catholicism' because that had a rather sectarian flavour). Thus I do not have to depend on memory or imagination for my beliefs at this time. Among the points I made was that it was a mistake to identify Catholicism with ritualism, that is, with a concern about the outward and ceremonial aspects of worship. We just took those things for granted and did not fuss about them at all. Another mistake was to suppose that Catholics wanted to return to the Middle Ages. That would be impossible anyhow. The Catholicism we stood for, though its essence was permanent and abiding – 'the faith once for all delivered to the saints' – had developed in the light of new discoveries and knowledge and was adapted to conditions in the contemporary world.

We stood for the restoration of communion with the universal Church and for repairing the schism that took place at the Reformation. Like Roman Catholics, English Catholics greatly prized the sacraments as means of grace. While we agreed with them 'in desiring to proclaim to the people of England . . . the way of salvation and sanctification through the full sacramental life' and while we were largely at one in our style of worship and the practice of the Christian life, we had 'a different intellectual outlook, a different attitude of mind' from the Roman Catholics. It seemed to us that 'this is the real weakness of the Roman Church that the intellectual fetters of its past make it so rigidly conservative, so nervous, and so proud, that it cannot and does not come to terms with new knowledge and new movements in our modern world'.

As regards Protestant nonconformity (as the Free Churches were then known), I said that 'we must recognize that they have produced in a remarkable way the fruits of Christian character and devotion', and that the blame for their separation was in part to be assigned to the Church of England itself. What had really led to their breaking away was the 'laxity, the low standard

48

of spirituality, which they found in the Church of their day.'
Still they should have worked for reformation from within the
Church, instead of breaking away from it. Catholics had much to
learn from Protestants, especially about the place of the Bible
in the Church and the importance of Bible-reading.

As regards the different groups or parties within the Church
of England itself which some regarded as a source of weakness,
I said that we should recognize that they all had a legitimate
place in the Church; none had a monopoly of truth. We could
distinguish different elements in each group. In the Low Church
there was the negative element which occupied itself in protest-
ing against what was catholic; but on the positive side there were
the evangelicals who were characterized by 'devotion to the
Bible, to the simplicity of the gospel, with their insistence on
freedom and reality in prayer, with their missionary zeal'.
Every true catholic ought to be an evangelical in this sense.

There were two elements also in the broad Church party. On
the one hand there were 'those timid, half-baked church-
people, whose motto is "no extremes" – "moderation, caution
at any price".' I had no sympathy with them. On the other hand,
the broad Church included a smaller group 'chiefly of scholars
who are called "modernists" or "liberals"', who were 'trying
to see and to state the truth as it is today; that is, to interpret
the faith of the church . . . in the language and thought of the
twentieth century'. This was a necessary task, though mistakes
would inevitably be made by those who took it in hand.

The professing Catholics in the Church instead of quarrelling
with or trying to controvert the other groups should get on
with positively witnessing to their beliefs in a disciplined and
costly way. In the history of the Church of England it was a
period of experiment, and we should trust that the truth would
prevail, if we all concentrated on what was positive in our
convictions. I may here have been influenced by a book that
S. C. Carpenter published at this time, entitled *A Large Room:
a plea for a more inclusive Christianity*. His theme, as I under-

stood it, was that in the Church of England we did not have to be catholic *or* evangelical *or* liberal, but we ought to be all three, and not moderately but thoroughly catholic *and* evangelical *and* liberal.

I leave this statement of my views in 1924 without comment. How far I maintained or modified them will become evident as we proceed. The only remark I would make at this point is that I would seem at that time to have regarded the fundamentals of belief – in the reality of God, etc. – as axiomatic and to have dealt with what was, however important, secondary. When later on I was called to work among students and to conduct university missions, I naturally had to start further back or deeper down.

The ordination retreat which I attended in December 1922 had been conducted by O. C. Quick, then a canon of Newcastle cathedral and later Regius Professor of Divinity at Oxford. I remember that he urged us not only to keep up our general reading in theology but to start specializing on some particular subject so that, if, for instance, we should be asked to read a paper to a group of clergy or to introduce a discussion, there would be some topic about which we would be likely to be better informed than other people.[1] We should also, he said, have more relish for study if we had such a special field of interest. I took his advice and decided to specialize on the study of the fourth gospel. During the next ten years I succeeded in procuring nearly all the major works on the subject in French and German as well as in English, and I constantly made detailed notes on the text of the gospel and whatever had to do with it. I went so far as to purchase an Aramaic grammar so that I might be able to judge the theory that St John's Gospel was

1. Mark Pattison gave this advice to Mrs Humphry Ward: 'Get to the bottom of something; choose a subject and know *everything* about it.'

originally written in that language. Although in the 1930s, when I was able to devote the bulk of my time to study and authorship, I did not go on with this specialism but entered other fields of research, I still think that Quick's advice was excellent. I have often passed it on to the newly ordained.

But I must not give the impression that my interests were all ecclesiastical or theological. The housing conditions and the appalling poverty that I encountered on Tyneside naturally enforced my socialism or at least my support for the Labour Party which seemed to be the only party that gave priority to improving such conditions. I have a copy (I fancy that very few are still in existence) of a 'Memorial of the Clergy to the Labour Members of Parliament' that was signed by over 500 Anglican clergymen in March 1923. The Labour Party had for the first time become the official opposition in the House of Commons: it was not foreseen that there would soon be a Labour government.

The 'Memorial' expressed satisfaction at the Party's success and looked forward 'to the more serious consideration and more adequate treatment of the pressing problems and difficulties of our time'. 'Our particular calling, with its pastoral experience, gives us direct knowledge of the sufferings and deprivation, mental, moral and physical, to which millions of our fellow citizens are subjected in our present social and industrial order, and to find remedy for which is the chief purpose and aim of the Labour Movement.' Many of the signatories of this 'Memorial' became known to me as time went on, and it would be interesting to ascertain how far they continued to support the Labour Party. Five of them became diocesan bishops.

There were two general elections during the two years that I worked in Newcastle. I forget how it started, but I was soon involved in political speaking and electioneering. I used to speak for Sir Charles Trevelyan who represented our constituency (Newcastle Central) and also for Sir Patrick Hastings over at Wallsend. I was given a seat on the platform when Ramsay Macdonald came to address a big pre-election meeting in the Palace Theatre. Sometimes on a Sunday evening I would dash off from a church service to speak at an ILP meeting, finding the atmosphere of the latter more exhilarating than the former. I always made it clear that I engaged in party politics as a citizen and not as a priest. My weekly reading included *The New Leader*, a socialist paper then being brilliantly edited by H. N. Brailsford, as well as *The Church Times*. I must say Ronald Wainwright was very indulgent to me, for he was a Conservative in politics and was working in the slums from a high sense of duty, whereas I would not have been anywhere else for worlds.

The Vicar of St Philip's parish, on the other hand, to which we were nominally attached though in fact we had very little to do with it, was a veteran Christian Socialist, W. E. Moll by name. He came to the parish in 1893 and as long ago as in 1895 had persuaded the Newcastle diocesan conference to pass a resolution that a decent wage should be the first charge upon products. He was still, when I knew him, idolized in the miners' lodges throughout Northumberland and Durham. In palmier days, before the First World War, St Philip's had been a very flourishing church; Moll's curates had included Conrad Noel and Percy Widdrington, both of whom were well-known Christian Socialists. Moll himself was a member of the Fabian Society.

By 1920 his congregation had fallen away and he had no curate. His interests appeared now to be political rather than religious. He was a friend of Ramsay Macdonald, who when he was Prime Minister nominated him to the Deanery of Carlisle, which Moll promptly accepted. But the appointment was so severely criticized that he found it expedient to get his medical adviser to tell him to withdraw his acceptance. Soon afterwards he was appointed to a valuable crown living where I was told he again became a model parish priest. I remember meeting Moll in the street one day and his telling me that the Prime Minister had asked him to meet him at the Central Station when he was passing through Newcastle, because he wanted to consult him about some ecclesiastical appointments: I even understood him to say that he had put in a good word for me, although I was at the time only a deacon!

In 1924 there was held in Birmingham a large interdenominational conference known as COPEC (conference on politics, economics and citizenship). It was presided over by William Temple and I should say that in effect it registered the acceptance by the churches in Britain of the idea that the Christian faith had social implications. In order to disseminate the message it was decided to follow up the Birmingham conference with a Northern COPEC Conference in Newcastle. L. S. Hunter, then a canon of the cathedral and later Bishop of Sheffield, was to be secretary, and he asked me to be assistant secretary. Thus I was much involved in it, and not only in the administration, for I remember making a speech in which I attacked one of the leading Tyneside shipowners face to face, and considerable heat was engendered. The most useful outcome of the conference was that it led to the appointment of an expert social scientist (H. A. Mess) to investigate conditions on Tyneside with a view to advising the churches what they could do to help meet the needs of the whole area.

However, most of my time in Newcastle was occupied with the normal employments of a parish priest, which of course embrace much more than preparing for and taking services. We were liable to be called to death-beds or other emergencies at any hour of the day or night. We were diligent in visiting and did some house to house visiting as well as attending to the needs of the sick and of church members. In Lent 1924 we had a week's special mission, conducted by Harold Dibben, who was then a member of the Oratory. In preparation for it every house in the district was visited by members of the church.

I was assigned to Buckingham Street, one of the longest and toughest. But it is idle to name streets, for since that time the whole area has been demolished, replanned and rebuilt.

We had a number of parish organizations, especially for young people. I acted as chaplain to the boy scouts and girl guides. I recall spending a week in camp at Felton in Northumberland, where the vicar was a kindly and simple soul. His surname had originally been Pig or Pigg. He changed it by deed-poll to Brown, which, we thought, showed a certain lack of inventiveness. I was also responsible for the catechism in church on Sunday afternoons to which a large number of children came, and I prepared boys for confirmation and first communion.

But I also had a reasonable amount of time for recreation and diversions. Wainwright subscribed to the civilized doctrine that priests should have the inside of a week away after Christmas and Easter and a month's holiday in the summer. I was able to maintain my existing friendships and to make new ones. I kept up an animated correspondence with Malcolm Muggeridge who stayed with us in Newcastle in the spring of 1924. He was still up at Cambridge. I often met Philip Strong who at Tyne Dock was within easy reach. Among the clergy on Tyneside whose friendship I valued I would mention J. S. Turnbull (known to his friends as 'T'). He had been curate of St John's, Newcastle, and was now Vicar of Seaton Hirst, a mining village where I stayed with him more than once. He was a northerner with a powerful mind. I profited much from discussing all sorts of questions with him. Later we had a summer holiday in Germany together and visited the Oberammergau Passion Play. He died at a comparatively early age in the 1930s.

Another congenial friend was Cyril Gardner: we had common intellectual and social interests. He was curate to C. E. Osborne at Wallsend to whom he introduced me. Osborne was by then a grand old man. He had written the life of Father Dolling and had been a close friend of Father George Tyrrell. I wish I had had the enterprise to draw on his reminiscences. I

remember during a debate in the Newcastle diocesan conference about prayer book revision Osborne's making the
caustic remark that Anglicans who talked about 'our incom-
parable liturgy' usually knew no other liturgy with which to
compare it! I should also like to have drawn on the reminiscences
of G. E. Newsome, then Provost of Newcastle and afterwards
Master of Selwyn, for he had known Baron Friedrich von
Hügel well.

My Cambridge friend Algy Robertson was near at hand:
indeed he was here, there and everywhere. He sorely tried his
vicar at St George's, Cullercoats, H. B. Fry, who was exceedingly
fastidious about punctuality and tidiness, but Algy with his
erratic habits and charm of manner and patent goodness got
away with irregularities which would not have been tolerated
in anyone else.

I had no desire to leave Newcastle. I should have been happy
to spend the rest of my working life on Tyneside and in
Northumberland, where there was a more friendly atmosphere
throughout the Church than I have found anywhere else. But
two years was a normal period for a first curacy, and it was
thought advisable that a young priest should widen his experience. In January 1923 I had become a priest-companion of
the Oratory of the Good Shepherd (which meant that the OGS
provided me with an appropriate rule of life upon the observance of which I reported periodically). My adviser was Wilfred
Knox, and it was he who suggested that I should move to
Birmingham where his friend, A. H. Barlee, needed a senior
curate. So I visited St Aidan's, Small Heath, and was attracted
by it. During my visit Barlee took me to a gathering of some
sort at Solihull which was addressed by the Bishop of Birmingham, Dr Russell Wakefield, who was on the point of retiring
– with unforeseen consequences!

I cannot leave Tyneside without recalling the clergy house
cat, Ignatius by name. He was a very pious cat, much addicted

to church attendance and to reposing in the pulpit. In fact he was so pious that on one Shrove Tuesday he greatly edified us by catching a mouse at five minutes before midnight so as not to break the Lenten fast which was better observed then than it is now.

CHAPTER V

Birmingham and Bishop Barnes

The parish of St Aidan's, Small Heath, had come into existence during the last decade of the nineteenth century in order to serve the rapidly increasing population of that part of Birmingham. There were about ten thousand parishioners. The housing conditions were not nearly so bad as those I had known in Newcastle, but some streets and alleys were bad enough with many back-to-back houses. However, a start was being made with building new housing estates on the outskirts of the city. As was the case with my Newcastle parish, most of St Aidan's parish, as I knew it, has now been demolished.

To begin with, St Aidan's Mission, as it was known, had a small temporary church together with a cottage where the missioner and his assistant lived. But these had soon been replaced by a permanent church and a clergy house that could accommodate three or four celibate priests. The exterior of the church was not impressive (it could be seen from the Great Western Railway as one entered Birmingham from London), but the interior was beautiful and it was well furnished. Built of brick and terra cotta, it is one of the best neo-gothic churches that I have seen, and it had that elusive quality described as atmosphere. It was a good place in which to pray and to worship or just to be still.

The church had prospered, served by a succession of gifted young priests, and also by Sisters of the Community of the Holy Name who resided in a converted shop and bakehouse. The congregation was mainly drawn from the parish or near neighbourhood, though some worshippers came from further

St Aidan's Church and Clergy House

afield, attracted by the character of the services. I think that by the time I joined the staff St Aidan's had seen its best days, though in most churches there are people who look back to the time of Father So-and-so and say that things have never been so good since. Certainly in my time (1924–31) the parish was busy enough. There were plenty of organizations for young and old and many kinds of activity going on day by day as well as the Sunday and weekday services.

The vicar, Father Barlee, was an Irishman, aged about fifty, who had previously worked in the east end of London and had also been Rector of St Paul's Cathedral, Rockhampton, in Queensland. He had only recently taken the place of C. N. Long, who had been Vicar of St Aidan's for about twenty years, was a much respected figure in Birmingham, and had gone to be warden of the diocesan retreat house. We saw quite a lot of him, and he was always ready to help in time of need, perhaps too ready for the comfort of his successor.

Barlee himself was the best type of Anglo-Catholic priest: he was devout, a good teacher and confessor, a tireless visitor of the sick and whole, free from fanaticism, and with a lively sense of humour. His principal recreations were driving a Trojan car and playing bridge on Sunday evenings. During his summer holiday he spent most of the time sending post-cards to his parishioners, though characteristically he would complain of the expense entailed by this practice. I admired but could not emulate the way in which he had lists of all the people whom since his ordination he had prepared for the sacraments or had ministered to in other ways, and prayed for them regularly by name. He was a genial companion even if he was somewhat peppery. He was most provoked by the housekeeper whom he had inherited from his predecessor. She was a cultured lady (I possess her copy of the Psalms in Greek) but more assiduous in caring for cats than in cultivating the culinary arts. She did not last for long. I shall have more to say later about some of her successors.

The other member of the staff, when I joined it, was Wilfrid

Westall who was then still a deacon. He is one of the most delightful people that it has been my good fortune to know: multitudes were to experience his charm and wit and his pastoral solicitude when he became Bishop of Crediton, if they had not done so before. He was already an ardent Devonian and an enthusiast for the Great Western Railway. We had much fun in the clergy house and I apprehend that the vicar often wondered what we would be up to next. After three years Wilfrid became engaged to a member of the congregation and moved to another parish. It was a tradition at St Aidan's that its priests should remain celibate while they were on the staff.

There was also room in the clergy house for one or two paying guests: it was a rule that they should attend mass on Sundays. I remember Max Trist, a very engaging and whimsical young man, who was wrapped up in motor cycling and may indeed have worked at the BSA in Small Heath. I should like to know what happened to him afterwards. Another shortlived paying guest was Malcolm Muggeridge. After leaving Cambridge he had gone to work in a missionary college in south India. We had kept up a regular correspondence (his side of which I have preserved) and in the course of it played a long drawn out game of chess which, I fear, in the end collapsed in confusion. When he returned to England in 1927 it was arranged that he should teach in an elementary school in Birmingham and reside in St Aidan's clergy house. His stay was shortlived not because we did not enjoy his company but because he soon became engaged to Kitty Dobbs. I was actually away on holiday when their marriage took place in a Birmingham registry office. I remember being somewhat shocked when Malcolm told me that they had at the same time inquired about how one got a divorce! As is well known, it in fact turned out to be one of the happiest and most steadfast unions that could be imagined.

I cannot say that I ever came to feel for the city of Birmingham what I had felt, and still feel, for Tyneside. But I became equally attached to those of its inhabitants among whom my lot was cast. I particularly relished the hospitality of our doctor

(John Notley) and his large, ebullient and quick-witted family and their relatives. Christmas days afterwards seemed tame in comparison with the parties in their house which always included a good spell of country dancing.

My memories of Birmingham are however sullied, if not dominated, by the fact that St Aidan's, and I myself, became involved in the ecclesiastical controversy that ensued upon the arrival in October 1924 of Dr E. W. Barnes as the new bishop. The controversy between Dr Barnes and his so-called rebel clergy attracted much publicity in the national press at the time, not least that part of it that centred on St Aidan's, but it is now quite forgotten. I will give as clear and concise (though naturally one-sided) an account of it as I can, not only because of the effect it had on my own life, but because it constituted a strange chapter in ecclesiastical history that should not disappear into oblivion.[1]

Dr Russell Wakefield, Barnes's predecessor, so far as I could make out, had been an easy-going, indulgent, and popular bishop, who had let his clergy do more or less what they liked in their churches, provided that they had the support of their people and were getting on with their job of ministering to the flock of Christ. This has always seemed to me a very sensible attitude, but it was not the attitude of Dr Barnes. He was better suited to be a don than a bishop. When I was leaving Newcastle, L. S. Hunter wrote to me knowingly: 'Would you like an introduction to your new bishop? He is an attractive man – though one could prophesy he would be a bad bishop as he is a don pure & simple.'[2] With his academic background he came

1. For my later and more balanced estimate of Dr Barnes and his episcopal proceedings I may refer to the centenary lecture that I gave about him in Birmingham Cathedral on 1 October 1974, which was published in *The Modern Churchman* (Spring 1975).

2. Wordsworth said of Dr Arnold of Rugby that he 'is a good man, an admirable schoolmaster, but he would make a desperate bad bishop'.

to Birmingham with a sense of mission. He conceived himself to be called, on the one hand, to take a leading part in adjusting the Christian faith to the discoveries of natural science and, on the other hand, to expunge from the churches in his diocese what he regarded as superstitious beliefs and practices. His disposition was such that, while in private he was a man of singular courtesy and grace, he never hesitated in public to say and to repeat harsh, wounding, and indeed outrageous things about those matters concerning which he felt strongly.

In other circumstances a bishop with these characteristics might have fastened on some other bone of contention. Barnes fastened on one that in the 1920s was being much discussed in the Church of England in connection with the revision of the Book of Common Prayer, namely the reservation of the sacrament of Holy Communion, that is, keeping the consecrated elements in a tabernacle or aumbry so that they were available at any hour of the day or night for giving communion to the sick or dying or to workers (such as nurses and milkmen) who were unable to be present at the ordinary times of service. This was a practice that had a long tradition behind it but there were differences of opinion (a) about how the sacrament when reserved should be treated, whether or not as an object of reverence and adoration symbolizing the presence of Christ (the eastern and western Churches had differed about this) and (b) whether the practice, which had admittedly fallen into disuse after the Reformation, was in fact inconsistent with the doctrine of the Church of England, and also whether it was permitted, or even required, by its formularies. When Bishop Barnes arrived he found that not only was the sacrament reserved in a considerable number of churches in his diocese, but in many of them it was used not only for giving communion but as a focus of devotion at extra-liturgical services.

Barnes was fond of saying that Holy Communion is a psychological process and that you cannot reserve a psychological process. It is true that Holy Communion is that, but it is also much more than that. As William Law said, 'the Sacrament is an *Abstract* or *Sum* of all the Mysteries that have been revealed concerning our Saviour'. The bishop was not however altogether consistent, for the rule that he decided to enforce so far as he could (pending a new decision by the Church in general) was that the sacrament might be reserved only if it were kept in an enclosed or curtained off chapel to which the public had no access. The incumbents of fifteen churches in the diocese (of which St Aidan's was one), supported by their church councils, refused to accept the bishop's ruling and to abandon the reservation of the sacrament in the open church to which they and their congregations were accustomed. They did not see why at the whim of an individual bishop they should give up a practice which was common and permitted in other dioceses and which reputable authorities held to be legal.

The incumbents of these fifteen churches therefore bound themselves to one another not to move or to resign their benefices so long as the bishop sought to enforce his idiosyncratic ruling. When, in consequence, the bishop treated them as rebels, refusing to visit their churches, or to license curates to them, or to allow them support from diocesan funds, they took steps, with the help of the English Church Union, to organize their own finances and with a good conscience engaged unlicensed curates when the need arose.

When I arrived in Birmingham towards the end of 1924, the lines of this controversy had not yet been drawn. I was the last curate to be licensed by the bishop to what was shortly to become a so-called rebel church. I remember at the licensing ceremony in the cathedral being surprised by the bishop's solemnly warning us that our assent to the Thirty-Nine Articles was to be taken with the utmost seriousness and rigour. It was by no means a formality, he said. He was of course thinking of those Articles (for example, no. xxviii) which appeared, or could be taken, to condemn what he looked upon as superstitious practices, but I knew well that he himself as a modernizing theologian sat lightly to some of the other Articles!

The controversy initiated by the bishop came to a head whenever a vacancy occurred in any of the parishes where the sacrament was reserved in the open church. He did not attempt to eject sitting incumbents from their livings, but he reckoned that if he waited long enough the so-called rebel vicars would sooner or later die or move or retire, and he would then take steps to see that their successors obeyed his ruling.

The first living to fall vacant in this way was St Mark's, Washwood Heath, and at St Aidan's we became involved in the trouble there. The first priest nominated by the patron, H. E. Bennett, lived with us at St Aidan's and helped us while the bishop was refusing to institute him, and we took the services at St Mark's. When he withdrew, since he would not accept the bishop's terms, the next nominee to my intense surprise was Ronald Wainwright under whom I had worked in Newcastle. What was to me still more surprising and disconcerting was that he agreed to accept Dr Barnes's ruling and so became the new Vicar of St Mark's. I did not scruple to tell Wainwright what I thought of his conduct in letting down our resistance to the bishop, but we became good friends again later.

I need not specify other episodes that occurred in the course of this tedious controversy, but will proceed at once to our own St Aidan's case which was the most protracted and dramatic of all. It arose out of the fact that Father Barlee became incapacitated by sciatica and the medical advice was that he must seek work in a warmer climate. After much searching of heart, he therefore sent in his resignation. The trustees, who were the patrons of the benefice and who included Bishop Frere of Truro, were determined to prevent the bishop from imposing his rule about the reservation of the sacrament on the new vicar. They therefore nominated a well-qualified priest who would decline to give the undertaking that Dr Barnes was sure to demand although he was not legally entitled to do so. This was G. D. Simmonds, who had been a fellow curate of Philip Strong at St Mary's, Tyne Dock. It was I who suggested his name to the trustees.

When, as was anticipated, the bishop refused to institute him, the trustees brought legal proceedings in the Chancery Division of the High Court of Justice in order to require him to do so. They succeeded in their case, but the bishop refused to obey the court's ruling. Further legal proceedings followed and eventually the court directed the Archbishop of Canterbury to institute our new vicar over the head of the Bishop of Birmingham. He was instituted by Archbishop Lang in Lambeth Palace Chapel on 7 July 1931, and I was among those present.

During the two years while these proceedings were taking place I was left as Priest-in-Charge of St Aidan's, though I had some help from C. N. Long and from a number of visiting priests. We managed to keep everything going. I remember one Sunday, before Barlee had finally left for the West Indies, a Singalese priest arrived to help. He was to be responsible for the first two of our four Sunday masses (at 7, 8, 10 and 11 a.m.). Before the first, at 7 a.m., he was taken ill in the sacristy. A member of the congregation who went to see what was amiss was astonished to find a coloured priest looking extremely sick, but had the composure to summon me from my bed. As I hurried into church I passed Barlee's bedroom. He was struggling to get out of bed in order to help: I peremptorily told him not to be a damned fool and embarked on the morning's labours. It was ironic that, when I started the third mass at 10 a.m., the first hymn to be sung was, by some inadvertence, 'Now the day is over'!

Though I have never been the incumbent of a parish, that is, a vicar or rector, my two years as Priest-in-Charge of St Aidan's gave me an equivalent experience. For instance, I was responsible for the parish magazine which I tried to brighten up by dropping the conventional 'Letter from the Vicar' and inserting instead imaginary interviews with prominent members of our congregation. I was also clerk or secretary of our ruri-decanal chapter: W. L. Anderson, afterwards Bishop of Salisbury, was the rural dean. I tried to brighten that up, too, by sending out what were intended to be humorous notices of forthcoming meetings. The following is one of my shortest and least allusive efforts:

> Bordesley Ruri-Decanal Chapter will meet on Tuesday September 24th 1929 at 4 p.m. at St Benedict's Vicarage, when the Reverend H. A. Jones will speak on 'Reunion: Is Anglicanism worth preserving?'
> It is hoped that you will be present.

Extract from PASTORS AT PLAY by the Reverend Dr Dolittle, ch. vi *The Clergyman's treat*, p. 74:

'The labourer in the ministerial vineyard, when wearied by the turmoil of the pastoral fray, will find unfailing solace in that joyous meeting with his brethren, which is known as *the ruri-decanal chapter*. Here brother clasps the hand of brother, and to the tune of merry quip and modest jest faces creased with care assume the radiance of a happy smile. No minister, young or old, should ever miss this grand opportunity of hearty fellowship, or rejuvenating uplift . . .'

Because of the tension among the clergy of different schools of thought and of my being regarded as a highly suspect rebel, these efforts of mine did not go down too well!

I naturally felt bound to stay at my post at St Aidan's until our new vicar had settled in. Otherwise I should doubtless have left Birmingham before this. I was, for instance, offered the chaplaincy of Downing College, Cambridge. Also I was invited to go out to India as unofficial chaplain to the Viceroy (Lord Irwin, afterwards Lord Halifax) and as tutor to one of his sons. But because of what seemed to me Dr Barnes's arbitrariness and obstinacy I was not free to consider such attractive propositions. There was the possibility that at any moment he might withdraw my licence to officiate. In order to be prepared for such a contingency I drafted a document that I still have which I intended to publish as a rejoinder. But happily I was left alone.

The congregation of St Aidan's rallied round and gave me

plenty of support and I do not think that the work of the parish suffered unduly during this awkward period. But I had my domestic adventures. When we needed a new verger for the church and a new housekeeper for the clergy house, the church-wardens and I advertised for a husband and wife who could jointly occupy those offices. The most plausible reply came from *two men*, who were recommended by an Anglo-Catholic priest in London and came for an interview. Both were bowler-hatted and both were bearded. The older man had a white beard, was blue-eyed and angelic-looking: he had kept house previously for Lady B. who was a vegetarian. As I myself was a vegetarian at that time, I was drawn to him. The younger man, who had a red beard, had a somewhat ferocious bearing, but appeared to be a possible verger: so we engaged them. This was in the autumn.

Things seemed to go well enough, though I thought the verger was rather brutal to the housekeeper. But I had some pleasant vegetarian dishes. The verger, in addition to the satisfactory performance of his duties, surprised us all by singing during services with quite unusual vigour and volume at the back of the church. On a morning in the spring, after saying mass, I came into the clergy house for my breakfast and found that they had both disappeared leaving no message or trace but only some pigeons which, without my knowledge, they had kept in the backyard. The puzzle was cleared up some weeks later when a member of our congregation was on top of a bus in London and, looking down, saw my erstwhile house-keeper, affecting to be blind, being led by the ex-verger who was doing a powerful turn as a street singer. This was evidently their way of earning a living in the summer, and they had made a convenience of us for the winter months!

We had to advertise again, and this time engaged a very nice unemployed miner from Merthyr Tydfil and his wife: they came into residence with their two boys and we became good friends. My study was over the front door of the clergy house. One morning I was at my desk when I was distracted by some flashing lights below. I looked out and discovered that the verger was being photographed by a bevy of press men. He had drawn a horse in the Irish Sweepstake, which was then an attraction for any who were disposed for an occasional flutter. The next morning he received about two hundred begging letters. We urged him to take legal advice about whether he should sell half his ticket. In the end he received enough money to tempt him to retire. This was after I had left Birmingham.

There were at the time some interesting repercussions. Dr Barnes was reported to have deplored that a church in his diocese should be mixed up with this kind of thing. It put me in a bit of a fix. I took a very strict view about the folly and iniquity of gambling and betting (a view which I have not modified much since): at the same time I wanted to stand by our verger. So I issued the following statement to the press:

It is unfair and hypocritical for ecclesiastical dignitaries to condemn a verger for a rare and occasional 'flutter', when rich men, whose wealth is the result of speculation, not only pass unrebuked, but are actively patronized by the Church. As a matter of fact the Church of England does not teach that betting and gambling are always absolutely wrong. Personally I wish the Church did teach this, and I hope that it will do so before long.

I may add that, although many churches and chapels allow raffles at their bazaars and sales of work, at St Aidan's we have always firmly refused to make money by such means.

Another embarrassing sequel was that the verger offered to make a presentation to the church as a thank-offering for his good luck. I had some difficulty in persuading our church council gratefully to decline the offer, while expressing appreciation of his intention.

In 1927–28 the long process of trying to secure authorization for a revised prayer book at last came to an end – at any rate for the time being. It ended in a fiasco, since after being approved by representative bodies of the Church it was twice rejected by parliament. Before being voted on by the convocations and the Church Assembly, it had been considered by the diocesan conferences. There was a majority for the new proposals in the Birmingham diocesan conference, but a minority that voted to the contrary was composed of the bishop and of his so-called rebels! The former was opposed to the revision because it conceded too much to Catholics, the latter because it did not concede enough! It can now be seen that the whole attempt at prayer book revision was misconceived from the start, since it was motivated by a desire to impose discipline in the Church by legal means, instead of by a desire to enable the Church to discover by judicious experiment what were the most appropriate forms of worship under contemporary conditions.

While purely ecclesiastical concerns inevitably occupied much of my time and interest during my seven years in Birmingham, I had plenty of other interests. In Newcastle I had been chaplain to a troop of boy scouts; at St Aidan's I became a scoutmaster. In order to qualify for this task, I went for an intensive ten-day course for scouters at Gilwell Park in Essex. I have never worked so hard nor learned so much in a period of that duration. Afterwards I did some written work and the outcome was that I was awarded the 'wood badge', a qualification much prized by scouters. It certainly enabled me to run the St Aidan's troop with confidence. We went to the international jamboree at Arrowe Park, Birkenhead, in 1929, and cheerfully endured the rain and the mud which were its most memorable features. I should have gone on with scouting (in which I am a firm believer) after I left Birmingham, if I had not had so many other employments.

I was a regular attender at the Birmingham Repertory theatre during these years, and was also a chaplain for the Actors' Church Union, which meant that once a week I visited the players behind the scenes, first at the Bordesley Palace, which was a variety theatre where spectacles such as the tallest and the shortest man in the world were displayed, and later at the

Alexandra Theatre. I was glad to do this, but a married chaplain with an attractive home to which he could invite actors and actresses would have been more effective. I do not know why I did not ask some of our more comfortably-off parishioners to help in that way.

While I continued to support the Labour Party, I did not find much time for political activity. On the Sunday during the general strike in May 1926 I preached a sermon that incurred the disapprobation of the Governor of the Bank of England in Birmingham who attended St Aidan's and who was liable to protest to the vicar about some of my utterances of a liberal or critical kind. For instance, when on one Whitsunday I said that we were not to suppose that on the day of Pentecost the apostles were miraculously endowed with a knowledge of foreign languages he complained of the contradiction between my sermon and the proper preface for Whitsunday in the prayer book which was sung later in the service and which declares that they were given 'the gift of divers languages'.

I had of course a regular summer holiday which I was prone to spend on the Continent as well as at my home in Rye or on a motor tour with my family. My father, like my vicar, owned a Trojan car. In 1927–28 he was Mayor of Rye. In that capacity, as well as being secretary of the local branch of the Royal National Lifeboat Institution, he was deeply concerned in the 1928 Rye Harbour lifeboat disaster when all hands were lost. He was instrumental in raising a sum of over £30,000 for the relatives and dependants, which, as is not uncommon in such cases, led to a lot of disagreeable quarrelling about how it should be distributed.

Although I had a great many other things to do, especially during the last two years when I was holding the fort single-handed, I continued to read a lot and reckoned normally to spend two hours a day in theological study. I have often used this experience in order to reprove clergymen who say that they cannot find any time for study. I also made my début as an author by publishing a course of sermons, entitled *Magic and Religion* (1930). Dr Barnes used to speak of Catholic priests as though they were the local magicians and he gave voice to monstrous generalizations about Catholic sacramentalism. My purpose was to show how and why his accusations were unwarranted and at the same time to provide some wholesome instruction in Christian doctrine. I was much gratified when many years later (in 1965) my friend J. S. Bezzant, who had also been a friend of Barnes and had indeed been invited to write his life, wrote as follows about this modest publication of mine:

> Had he (Barnes) carefully read Alec Vidler's four sermons, though he may not have modified his administrative orders to his resisting priests, I should like to believe that he would not have continued to condemn their teaching in language which made harmonious relations impossible. Thus, fairly early in his ministry, Vidler contributed one of the few things in an unhappy controversy which one can recall without regret (*Theology*, lxviii. 20).

During my last year in Birmingham I was more ambitious and produced a book entitled *Sex, Marriage and Religion: a discussion of some modern problems* (1932). The Lambeth Conference of 1930 occasioned much public disputation about matrimonial questions, especially contraception, and I was constantly confronted with them in the course of my ministry, especially in the confessional. I embarked on this book in order to clear my own mind. Reading it again after an interval of more than forty years, I am struck by the amount of good sense and persuasive argumentation that it contained, though naturally there are arguments I should now want to qualify and conclusions I should want to modify. My appeal throughout was to experience and reason, not to tradition and authority. I endeavoured to give a fair statement of the case for what was then called 'the new morality' and is now called 'the permissive society', before stating the objections to it. It may have been this that led the reviewer in the *Birmingham Post* to write: 'Mr Vidler brings to his task a broadness of outlook apparently so detached from all conventional dogmas that at times one can scarcely believe the book to be the work of a celibate priest of the Church of England.'

Nevertheless, my conclusions were not particularly unconventional. I argued against divorce and extra-marital sex, but for the permissibility of the use of contraception within marriage. Less conventional was my insistence on seeking equality of status, especially economic status, for women and a plea that not only celibates but married people could be called to the life of the counsels or to the so-called 'religious' life. But there is no point in going on about this book, as any unsold copies were destroyed by Hitler's bombers early in the war.

When all is said and done, my happiest memories of St Aidan's are of the children and young people with whom I had most to do and with whom I was most at home. I cannot forbear to quote a farewell letter from one of them (aged 12) which I did not deserve but which it is pleasant to have received and to have retained:

Dear Father Vidler,

Will you please accept this small gift I have sent you, to keep in memory of me. I have paid for it myself, and chosen it myself, and I know that you will think as much of it, as if it was a big present. I wanted to give you something quite by myself, because I shall never forget you, and shall always remember how very kind and jolly you were to me. We shall all of us miss you very and I hope that if you take any more children that they will all love you like the children from St Aidan's. Mother said that I must not say Good bye as we shall always be pleased to see you whenever you come to Birmingham. Thanking you for all your kindness. I shall never forget you. Please don't forget me will you?

Love and XXXXXXXXXXXXX from Barbara.

I received another farewell letter, of a different kind. By the end of September 1931 Father Simmonds had settled in as Vicar of St Aidan's and would be able to get a new, though unlicensed, curate; so I was free to move to Cambridge for the beginning of the Michaelmas term which, for reasons that I will presently explain, I wanted to do. I therefore wrote to tell Dr Barnes that I should be leaving Birmingham (without mentioning that I had put in seven years of tolerably hard work in his diocese). He replied as follows:

Dear Mr Vidler,
   I thank you for your letter of August 21 informing me that you propose to leave the Diocese early in October next. Will you allow me to urge that in any Diocese to which you may go you should carefully keep the pledge which you make in taking the Oath of Canonical Obedience.
                    Yours sincerely,
                    E. W. BIRMINGHAM

This communication seemed to me to be so remarkable that I at once had it framed and it has adorned the walls of my study ever since.

CHAPTER VI

At the Oratory House

I have already made mention of the Oratory of the Good Shepherd and of the Oratory House at Cambridge (see p. 38), where I had resided for six months in 1922. I must now say something more about both. During the 1920s the OGS had been growing in membership (perhaps too rapidly) both at home and abroad. The members were organized, in so far as they were organized, in groups known as 'colleges' (a rather misleading term) or 'chapters'. Those in each college or chapter lived and worked within sufficiently easy reach of one another to make a corporate observance of the Rule possible, but they were not necessarily under the same roof. In Cambridge, as I explained, some lived together in the Oratory House while others lived in the colleges of the university in which they held appointments. There was also provision for individual members, called 'mission brothers', who observed the Rule and maintained contact with an Oratory centre but who lived further afield. I had been accepted as such a member while I was still at St Aidan's, Small Heath, and had made my first profession on 12 January 1927. I had also often paid visits to the Oratory House.

The OGS in Cambridge had experienced what might have been a serious setback when its first superior and the Warden of the Oratory House, John How, had resigned his membership in order to marry (he was later to become Primus of the Scottish Episcopal Church). His place as superior had been taken by Eric Milner-White, Dean of King's College, who was a founder-member. Wilfred Knox became Warden of the Oratory

House. By 1931 it came about that he was the only member actually in residence at the house, and if its work was to go on it was urgently necessary that one or two other members should join him there. It was therefore decided that, as soon as I was free to leave Birmingham, I should move to Cambridge, and that at the same time another (senior) member of OGS, William Lutyens, should do the same. So from 1931 to 1938 we three were resident in the house while from time to time other members stayed with us for longer or shorter periods.

William Lutyens, who was a brother of Sir Edwin Lutyens the well-known architect, had as a young man held the world record for running the mile, and had then naturally been more famous than his brother. But athletic fame is more transitory than that of an architect. William had been a much loved parish priest for most of his life; he was also something of a poet and an author of devotional works.

The Oratory House, Lady Margaret Road, was a substantial building at the northern end of the Backs. Our neighbours were Westminster College (which always had a staff of distinguished Presbyterian theologians) and Dr F. R. Tennant, the eminent philosophical divine who was a keen gardener. He could be seen any day attending to his rockeries.

When I moved to Cambridge, a hut in our garden served as our chapel, but very soon a new chapel, with two altars, was built on to the hosue, in which we met for the daily offices of the Church that in those days were customarily said in religious communities. Although the OGS did not purport to be a religious community of the same kind as orders of monks or friars, it aimed at providing a means by which unmarried men might live an ordered life in fellowship with one another while doing ordinary jobs in the world. We were, as far as was practicable, committed to the life of the counsels.[1]

1. i.e., poverty, chastity and obedience. For a positive exposition of what these negative-sounding ideas or ideals imply, see H. A. Williams C.R., *Poverty, Chastity and Obedience: the true virtues* (1975).

As regards chastity, we were pledged to celibacy as long as we remained members: the Rule did not permit us to pledge ourselves for life till we had been members for at least ten years (I made my life-profession in 1939). We could not all be vowed to poverty in the strict sense, but we all had to keep a detailed account of our income and expenditure and regularly to submit our accounts for inspection and criticism, and those of us who lived in an oratory house shared a common purse, each receiving just a small allowance for out-of-pocket expenses. While we could not practise the kind of obedience rendered by monks to their abbot, we were bound to consult the Oratory about any important decision we had to make (for example, about change of work) and to report to our fellow-members on our daily observance of the Rule, the provisions of which we kept to ourselves and disclosed only to *bona fide* inquirers. I have been writing in the past tense, but the OGS, unlike some religious communities, is still what it was in 1931, and I am still a grateful, though unworthy, member; in fact I am now the oldest member both in age and in length of profession.

So much as regards the OGS itself, which at present has between forty and fifty members in different parts of the world. The Oratory House at Cambridge is another matter (confusion was caused when it was spoken of as 'The Oratory'). It was a particular undertaking of the members in Cambridge which lasted for about twenty years. As I have said, it served three main purposes. It served as a centre for the OGS in Cambridge, for those who resided in colleges of the university as well as for those actually residing in the house; moreover, members overseas, when they were on leave, came and stayed with us, and when numbers were not too large the annual general chapter was held there. Then it was also a house of study. I shall soon have something to say about the theological work in which Wilfred Knox and I were engaged. In addition we always had a number of post-graduate research students or visiting scholars living with us. Thirdly, the Oratory House became most widely known because of its pastoral work among undergraduates, of whom we got to know a great many.

Some were commended to us by relatives or friends when they came up as freshmen; they in turn would bring their friends along to meet us. Further, we had the use of St Edward's church in the centre of Cambridge for a sung mass on Sunday mornings at which in term time the members of OGS preached courses of sermons and which was attended chiefly by undergraduates. Finally, we made many contacts through the Cambridge Mission to Fruitpickers for which we were responsible and on which I must enlarge in a moment. On nearly every evening in term time the three of us who were resident in the Oratory House had an undergraduate to dine with us, and we kept open house at tea time and on other occasions. Thus a considerable part of our time was occupied in personal conversations, mostly about questions of religion and morality.

The Cambridge Mission to Fruitpickers, familiarly known as the Fruiting Campaign, had been started in 1912 by John How and others as a way by which undergraduates could be of use to the thousands of fruitpickers who came every summer from east London and Sheffield to the area round Wisbech to pick strawberries and other fruit. I have a photograph of E. W. Barnes (then a tutor of Trinity College) on the campaign in 1914, wearing a straw hat and seated in a donkey cart! The pickers, who regarded their visit to the fruit farms as a holiday as well as a means of making money, were housed in rough shanty dwellings like the hoppickers in Kent. Few amenities were provided for them. Each year the Fruiting Campaign set up about half a dozen camps with a view to covering as much of the area as possible. Each camp had about six undergraduates under canvas and three or four students from the women's colleges who were housed in a local school or parish hall and acted as nurses.

During the daytime each camp had a crèche for the pickers' children, many of whom were still babies; they were looked after while their parents were out picking. In the evenings there would be entertainments of one kind or another, while some campaigners, especially medical students, visited the outlying farms and attended to the needs of pickers who were afflicted by bad sunburn, by the strawberry back and other ailments. So far as possible each camp had a chapel of sorts and a chaplain, either a member of OGS or another priest from the university. There was a daily mass and compline was said before the campers settled down for the night. On Sundays there were services and Sunday schools for the pickers and their children, and on Saturday afternoons and evenings the Campaign transferred its activities to the town of Wisbech into which the pickers flocked for their weekly shopping. The Corn Exchange was made available for their comfort and refreshment. In the evening we did some open-air preaching in the town, and then two or three of the chaplains would go 'progging', that is, would walk around as the university proctors used to do, each attended by two 'bull-dogs', seeking to quell any outbreaks of rowdiness, picking up drunks and getting them back to their farms, and so on.

The Campaign lasted for approximately six weeks from mid-June to the latter part of July. There were about a hundred campaigners each year; some stayed for the whole time, others came for a week or a fortnight (I myself had spent a fortnight on the Campaign when I was an undergraduate). We all cycled or drove into Wisbech each day for lunch which had to be served in two sittings so that the camps were not left unstaffed; otherwise we fended for ourselves. It was certainly a good experience for undergraduates to organize such an undertaking and to get to know and befriend the pickers and their children in a natural and easy way. The campaigners also got to know one another well; many lasting friendships were made; and the presence of the 'nurses' and the discovery of their skills led to some happy marriages.

Every year from 1932 to 1938 I was present for the whole

Campaign. In 1932 I took the opportunity of growing a beard. I had a motor bicycle and my own tent that I called 'The Manse', a lovely word of which I did not think Scottish and dissenting ministers should have a monopoly. At first Wilfred Knox was the senior chaplain, but after a year or two he handed over that responsibility to me. It was not only during the Campaign that my time was occupied with its concerns. There were frequent meetings and 'squashes' for campaigners in Cambridge with a view to recruiting for the next year and to raising funds. Also during each Christmas vacation we had reunions for the pickers both in east London and in Sheffield. Altogether I enjoyed my part in the Fruiting Campaign more than anything else during these years in Cambridge. I was able to recapture some of the satisfaction of the pastoral work in the parishes in which I had previously served.

However, I will not deny that I also enjoyed during most of the year having plenty of time for study and writing, especially during university vacations. When I returned to Cambridge in 1931 Wilfred Knox was already at work on a book to be entitled *The Development of Modern Catholicism* which was intended to mark the centenary of the Oxford Movement of 1833. It set out to show how in the course of a hundred years a movement that started with a thoroughly conservative and backward-looking orientation had by degrees become open to new forms of knowledge and new ways of thinking and was now thoroughly critical as well as thoroughly catholic. Wilfred invited me to collaborate with him by doing some research and writing for chapters that he had not yet drafted, and I was glad to do so. But it was extremely generous of him to insist on treating me as joint-author of the book since I had only a minor part in its composition. In any case Wilfred was much more erudite than I could ever be, particularly in the fields of classical and early Christian literature. My own interests by this time were chiefly in modern Church history where indeed they have remained.

It may be that I was of some use to him in other ways. He

was not only an Oxford man but was shy and retiring, and I found that, although he had already published a large and learned work about St Paul, he had not at all become involved in the life of Cambridge University and was not even making use of the university library. I was able to begin to remedy this state of affairs, a process that was carried further by another member of OGS, Edward Wynn, tutor of Pembroke College, by whose offices Wilfred became a member of that college of which later he was to be made a fellow.

My impression is that during the 1920s and 1930s Wilfred's ecclesiastical sympathies and his theological stance, which when I first knew him seemed to be narrowly, if not exclusively, Anglo-Catholic, were steadily broadening. This was in part due no doubt to his membership of the Archbishops' Commission on Christian Doctrine which after fifteen years' work produced its report, *Doctrine in the Church of England*, in 1938, a report that was manifestly influenced by the Cambridge members of the commission. Wilfred's opinions in the field of biblical criticism were also becoming more radical, some would say more sceptical. I remember when our mutual friend, John Collins (then Vice-Principal of Westcott House), was lunching with us one day, Wilfred announced somewhat portentously that it was a notable day in the history of New Testament scholarship as he had that morning finally decided that the Epistle to the Ephesians was not written by St Paul. John completely deflated the announcement by saying: 'Good heavens, have you only just realized that?' Never before or afterwards did I see Wilfred so nonplussed for a piece of repartee!

We had hardly completed the typescript of *The Development of Modern Catholicism* when in May 1932 it was made known that the subject for the Norrisian prize essay in the university was to be 'The origins and outcome of the modernist movement condemned by the encyclical *Pascendi gregis*'. The Norrisian prize (worth over £100) was the most valuable prize open to theologians and was awarded only once in five years. I doubt if I should have had the temerity to go in for it, had it not been that the subject was one to which I was already drawn. I had for some time been collecting literature about the Roman Catholic Modernists, and had visited their most renowned survivor, M. Alfred Loisy, in September 1931. I therefore set to work and produced a substantial essay which earned me the prize. It made a book of nearly 300 pages which was published by the Cambridge University Press in 1934 with the title, *The Modernist Movement in the Roman Church*. I think I may say without immodesty that it became the standard work on the subject in English. I have commented on its genesis and reception in the 'autobiographical introduction' to my later work *A Variety of Catholic Modernists*, so that I need say no more about it here.

I put a good deal of work into my share of the courses of addresses which members of the Oratory gave each term in St Edward's church, and also into various lectures and papers that I was invited to prepare on theological subjects, mainly for undergraduate societies. After a few years I found that I had sufficient material of this kind to make up a book that would deal with the principal themes of Christian belief. I called it *A Plain Man's Guide to Christianity: essays in liberal Catholicism* (1936). It contained four parts: I. Belief in God; II. Belief in Christ; III. The Church and the Means of Grace; and IV. Last Things. In the introduction I said: 'I hope this volume may do something to remove the widespread impression that Christianity is bound up with a rigid intellectual conservatism, with obsolete views of the world, with an antiquated attitude to the Bible, and with a narrow and exclusive ecclesiastical temper.' It was on the whole favourably received. *The Green Quarterly* treated it as the 'Book of the Season', A. S. Duncan Jones, the Dean of Chichester, being kind enough to say of it:

Mr Vidler's book pins the reader down to definite intellectual problems and leaves no room for vagueness. It covers the whole gamut of Christian faith, and it does so with a lucidity of style that is saved from aridity by just the requisite warmth at important points. It is an appeal to reason that is not afraid to recognize that life, not speculation, is the thing to be reasoned about. It is based throughout on an appeal to experience, not to abstract logic nor to dogmatic premisses.

Perhaps I should remark here upon what is probably obvious enough, namely that I am no metaphysician. I used to read quite a lot of metaphysics, but it seemed to me that philosophers of that sort, while some wrote more or less clearly, or more or less obscurely, than others, were, to speak generally, all equally clever and equally skilful at refuting one another. If I had to opt for a philosophy, it would be for the so-called 'pragmatism' of C. S. Peirce, William James, F. C. S. Schiller, Edouard Le Roy, etc. I know that the professionals are wont to speak disparagingly of 'pragmatism', but I have noticed that when it comes to the point they nearly all act upon it. I came to the conclusion that inescapably I had the cast of mind of an historian, not of a metaphysician. I admit that it is a lowlier cast of mind and I accept what Dr Johnson said about it:

> Great abilities are not requisite for an Historian; for in historical composition all the greatest powers of the human mind are quiescent. He has facts ready to his hand; so there is no exercise of invention. Imagination is not required in any high degree; only about as much as is used in the lower kinds of poetry. Some penetration, accuracy, and colouring will fit a man for the task if he can give the application which is necessary (Boswell, *Life of Johnson,* ed. Croker, 1844, ii. 207f.).

But, to return to the sequence of events, in the following year Wilfred Knox and I collaborated in the production of another book which consisted of lectures and addresses that we had been giving. Its title was *The Gospel of God and the Authority of the Church* (1937) and it enlarged upon theses that we had already adumbrated in our earlier writings. By this time reviewers and others regularly described us as representatives of 'the Cambridge school of liberal Catholicism'. This was in part a reference back to the Cambridge contributors to *Essays Catholic and Critical* (see p. 47), and in part a recognition of the fact that a number of us in Cambridge were working out a type of Christian apologetic that had a certain coherence and distinctive character. It based its case not on the oracular infallibility of a pope or a church but on empirical evidence, i.e. the totality of Christian experience throughout the ages. It owed something to a book by Will Spens, viz. *Belief and Practice* (1915), a book that was rich in thought but poor in style. He was now Master of Corpus and a close friend of Wilfred Knox. Among others who were regarded as members of this school of thought were Eric Milner-White and C. P. Hankey, Vicar of St Mary the Less, Cambridge. It was, I believe, Spens who as Vice-Chancellor at the time was responsible for setting the subject of my Norrisian prize essay and he seemed to be much pleased with the result. Kenneth Ingram, a publisher and the editor of *The Green Quarterly*, was our chief publicist.

While I suppose I felt flattered to be looked upon as one of the younger and promising members of this school of thought, I was never altogether happy about it. I had an ever-increasing dislike for being labelled and for being identified with any reputed sect or party within the Church. In 1930, before I left Birmingham, when another Anglo-Catholic Congress was being held in London, I had publicly dissociated myself from it. As will appear shortly, when occasion offered I struck out on a line of my own.

Meanwhile, I appear to have been acquiring some repute as a preacher, though I do not know how or why. I was frequently being asked to preach in colleges and schools. In 1935 I conducted a parochial convention at St Mark's, Washwood Heath, in spite of the fact that when Dr Barnes was informed of the project he had written to the vicar (Ronald Wainwright): 'I *will not* have Mr Vilder to preach in this diocese.' Then in 1937 I was invited to take a leading part in a mission to Oxford University that was being planned for the Hilary term 1938 and to give the main course of addresses in the university church.

The invitation, which was supported by the deans and chaplains, came through the vicar, F. A. Cockin, for some reason always known as George Cockin. I had not known him before but we became fast friends, and I was much indebted to him for help in preparing for the mission, for commenting on the drafts of my addresses, and for very acceptable hospitality. The other missioners were J. H. Linton (formerly bishop in Persia), A. C. Craig (Chaplain of Glasgow University), John How (then Vicar of Brighton), and J. R. Coates (of the Selly Oak colleges).

The mission took place from 29 January to 6 February 1938. I had to speak at the opening meeting on the first Saturday evening, at which the Vice-Chancellor presided, and then to give an address each evening throughout the week. I was available during much of each day for interviews and hearing confessions, and in fact was kept so busy in this way that I had to stay on in Oxford till the middle of the following week. Never before or since have I had such an awareness of the Holy Spirit's activity and of myself as simply an unworthy agent as I had during this mission. If any human credit is due it is to the many people who supported it with their prayers. For example, I had a message from Westcott House, Cambridge, to say that the students there were keeping an all-night vigil of prayer on our behalf.

The Record newspaper, which as an organ of evangelicalism thought most highly of Bishop Linton as a missioner, nevertheless published this generous report:

85

There can be no doubt that by far the greatest numbers were attracted to St Mary's. There the Rev. A. Vidler spoke to some 500 to 600 men each night. His approach was doctrinal and appealed to men seeking an intellectual basis for faith. Everyone is agreed that his addresses were characterized by clarity of thought and keen awareness of present thought movements and intellectual difficulties. He gave full weight to the attractions of the many rivals to Christianity for men's allegiance, only to show in the end where they ran counter to Christ and his claims. It was this attractiveness of manner and fairness of presentation which held his audience throughout the week.

My addresses were published as a book in the Christian Challenge Series, and entitled *God's Demand and Man's Response* (1938). In re-reading them today I was wondering how far they would indicate what I know to be the case, that in the latter part of the 1930s I was much influenced by the teaching of Reinhold Niebuhr. Although I did not mention him by name, it is clear that he had already weaned me from the idealistic, perfectionist, pacifistic, Utopian ideas with their confidence in the possibility of secular progress by which, like many others, I had been led astray after the First World War. However, the influence of Niebuhr is much more evident in the next book I wrote, after I had left Cambridge: so I defer further comment on this matter till I come to that.

But before I describe the circumstances that led to my departure from the Oratory House I will say something about our manner of life there and about some of my diversions. We each had a large bed-sitting-room which we looked after ourselves. We also waited on ourselves at meals, having a rota of duties for the purpose, but the food was produced by domestics in the background. We were responsible for the large flower garden; an area set apart for vegetables was looked after by an elderly gardener named Puller, to whom we always referred as 'Father Puller' after the well-known Cowley Father of that name. Wilfred Knox had become a dedicated horticulturist, having been instructed by the New Testament scholar, B. T. D. Smith, a one-time member of OGS and then tutor of Sidney Sussex College. In my early years at the Oratory House I worked in the garden on nearly every afternoon under Wilfred's direction; undergraduates were sometimes roped in to help us. I owe my enduring zest for gardening and most of what I know about it to this experience. Later I eased off somewhat since I did not regard it as the best way of using my time, and I went for walks with undergraduates instead.

The annual retreat (usually at Malling Abbey in Kent) and general chapter of the Oratory were held in the latter half of August, and as the long vacation term kept us in Cambridge till then it was not until September that we were able to take a holiday. Among the holidays that I recall with special pleasure was one in Switzerland with the Muggeridges in 1933 when they had just come out of Russia in revulsion against the Stalinist regime. It was on this occasion that Malcolm asked me to baptize his children: intending it, I think, as an anti-communist gesture. I refused to do so, because at that time he was not willing to undertake that they should be brought up in the Church. But in the long run Malcolm's wish was to be fulfilled more amply than he or I could have foreseen: by various routes his children all became fully committed Christian believers and in due time their families too.

In 1936 I had another holiday with Malcolm and Kitty in Donegal when we attended a *ceilidh* and acquired a taste for visiting Ireland; at least I did, and Ireland was to become more accessible to me when I moved to North Wales. In 1937 Malcolm and I spent a week or so in France. I remember that we detrained at Lisieux but were so appalled by the commercialization of the memory of the Little Flower that we took the next train for Paris, where he wanted to look up a descendant of Wordsworth's natural daughter.

In September 1935 I had had the use of a cottage in the Lake District above Boot in Eskdale, and three undergraduate friends stayed with me there. The weather was unfavourable and in order to divert ourselves we assumed the characters of a party of Rumanians. I was a Count (Ratalescu by name) with my son and nephew and an English undergraduate to act as interpreter. Whenever on our walks we met strangers the interpreter would warn them that in accordance with Rumanian custom the Count would offer them snuff and would be mortally offended if they did not take it! I have always had a flair (which I learned from my mother) of talking gibberish that sounds like a foreign language, and my son and nephew did their best with the same accomplishment. The interpreter had the hardest task. One evening we went to a local hotel and called for cards with a view to playing bridge, only to find that because of other company we would not be able to call or to converse intelligibly! We raised our glasses to King Carol and threw them out of the window or appeared to do so. A hotel guest who had been watching us without suspecting the truth got up at length and, bowing to me profoundly, said, *Gute Nacht*, which was doubtless the nearest he could get to Rumanian!

In March 1938 John Collins and I paid what turned out to be our last visit to Alfred Loisy at his home at Ceffonds in France. We stayed there for two days and had four long conversations with him. I made a careful record of what he said, which has recently been published in the *Journal of Theological Studies* (April 1977). In those days I used to wear an Irish policeman's inverness-style rain coat which I had bought secondhand and to which I was much attached though it made me look like a tramp. Anyhow, on the way home we had to change trains at St Dizier and went into the station buffet for some refreshment. It was crowded with working-men seated at tables. As I walked among them looking for a place and holding an old cloth cap upside down in my hand, they started throwing *sous* into it, which made it hard for us to retain our composure!

I also visited Rye two or three times a year and was able to be at home for Christmas. In 1934 my sister was married to an old family friend, and my father published *A New History of Rye* for which he had been gathering information and doing research for many years. In 1936 my mother, whose health had been failing, died on 20 July; what I owed to her is immeasurable. My father, who was a handyman out of doors, was no good at looking after himself indoors and was fortunately able to get a housekeeper. He always had a dog though he was not at all adept at training or controlling them.

The series of events and considerations that led to my departure from the Oratory House (but not of course from the Oratory) is somewhat complicated. On 30 November 1937 I received from Dr Lowther Clarke, editorial secretary of SPCK, an unexpected inquiry whether I would consider an invitation to edit the monthly journal *Theology*. This had been founded in 1920 as, in effect, an organ of English liberal Catholicism, and had been successfully edited by E. G. Selwyn, who had also edited *Essays Catholic and Critical*. In 1933 he handed over the editorship to my former tutor, S. C. Carpenter, who had written graceful editorials, but in other respects had not been a good editor. Lowther Clarke told me that Carpenter answered only one out of ten of his letters, and was liable to leave packets of manuscripts in the train. The circulation had been going down and although Carpenter had not yet resigned SPCK anticipated that he would be willing to do so.

This inquiry, for at first it was no more than that, brought to a head various considerations that had been exercising my mind. From my undergraduate days I had had the feeling that sooner or later I ought to work overseas, but whenever an opportunity or plan to do so had looked like materializing it had always been blocked in one way or another. While at the Oratory House I had been offered or approached about two or three overseas bishoprics, but the Oratory decided (I am sure, rightly) that my aptitudes, such as they were, suited me better for work at home than abroad. On the other hand, I was not disposed to continue much longer my work at the Oratory House. For one thing, I was getting bogged down in too many activities. In addition to those I have already spoken of, I was senior friend to the Student Christian Movement in Cambridge (which was then a large and flourishing organization), I was Chaplain to the Guild of St Bernard in Queen's College, and a member of several groups and committees.

Furthermore, I had come to believe that it would be in the best interest of the Oratory if I left Cambridge and started another OGS centre elsewhere. Whereas in the 1920s the membership had been increasing, in the 1930s it had been shrinking. I put this down to the fact that because of the Oratory House and our association with Cambridge, together with our theological writings, the idea had got around that the OGS was an academic society that stood for a special school of religious thought, whereas in my view it was (or ought to be) more calculated to appeal to parish priests and others who wanted a fellowship under a rule of life, but were not necessarily at all academically inclined. Therefore I favoured some break away from Cambridge, even if it meant handing over the Oratory House to some other agency.

When Will Spens and others had suggested to SPCK that I might edit *Theology* they certainly assumed that I would continue to be in Cambridge, that I would make it an organ of Cambridge liberal Catholicism, and that as editor I would be guided by their advice. But I was by no means prepared to undertake the task on those terms. I judged that I must get away from Cambridge and make a fresh start if I was to do this job. I would not want to edit the journal as an organ of any single group, but would give it a much wider base, and select my own body of advisers and collaborators. As I have explained in *20th Century Defenders of the Faith* (p. 80), 'Spens, who was a canny Scot and a master of diplomacy, was not at all pleased with the outcome of his manoeuvre.'

SPCK, however, was attracted by my plans, but as the editor's stipend was to be only £100 per annum there remained the question, if I were to leave the Oratory House, how and where I was to live and do the editorial work. Lowther Clarke hereupon resuscitated an idea that had been canvassed when *Theology* had originally been founded, namely that it should be sponsored by St Deiniol's Library, Hawarden, and that the editor should live there free of charge. The trustees of St Deiniol's welcomed the proposal, and so did I, especially as the then Warden of the library was going shortly to retire and there was a distinct possibility that I might be appointed to succeed him. The Oratory, after some initial doubts, eventually approved this plan. It was agreed that the Oratory House should be handed over to the Society of St Francis, that William Lutyens should accompany me to Hawarden, and that Wilfred Knox should be re-housed in Cambridge where there would still be three or four other members of OGS in residence in the university. Thus it came about that I was free to move to Hawarden on 5 October 1938 and to set forward my preparations for taking over the editorship of *Theology*.

CHAPTER VII

St Deiniol's Library and the Second World War

I arrived in Hawarden just after the Munich agreement by which, I may say, I was neither elated nor deceived. For some time the villagers took me to be a Czech refugee, no doubt because of my sartorial irregularity: I was still wearing my Irish policeman's outfit. St Deiniol's Library is a unique institution, the last and perhaps the most enduring product of Mr Gladstone's fertile mind. In the latter part of the nineteenth century everyone had heard of Hawarden, for the castle there was his home. Nowadays it is less well known, although Sir William Gladstone, the present owner of the estate, is the Chief Scout. I must describe the foundation of St Deiniol's in some detail, before recording my association with it and the part it played in my life.

Towards the end of his long career Mr Gladstone conceived the admirable idea of making his large library, which contained about 30,000 volumes, available for future generations of students. It was to be a residential library, that is, one in which people who wanted to make use of it could reside for longer or shorter periods. There was to be a body of a dozen trustees who were to have the oversight of the foundation, and a warden who would be responsible for its day-to-day administration. While he was to be in Anglican Orders, it was laid down in the trust deed that there were to be no religious tests for users of the library; it would be open to all *bona fide* readers whatever their religious or political beliefs. The library, to which additions would regularly be made, covered most of the humanities, but not the natural or mechanical sciences.

During his last years Mr Gladstone himself presided over the transfer of his books from Hawarden Castle to temporary buildings on a site in the centre of the village, adjoining the parish church, and his son-in-law, Harry Drew, became the first warden. After the GOM's death a large permanent stone building was erected, one side of which housed the library, and the other side was a residential hostel. There were plenty of grounds and gardens, and visitors were given access to the extensive park and woods surrounding the castle. St Deiniol's itself was finely situated with a view over the Dee estuary and Wirral, and on a clear day Liverpool could be seen.

The charges for residence were very moderate since they were eased by endowments. The staff included a sub-warden and matron and a complement of domestic servants. Later the trustees arranged for the annual election of three Gladstone research students, one from Oxford, one from Cambridge, and one from the modern universities. Among those who held Gladstone studentships in the course of the years I may mention Dr David Thomson (the late Master of Sidney Sussex College, Cambridge); Mr Ivor Bulmer-Thomas; Dr Noel Davey (sometime sub-warden); Professors Christopher Evans (the New Testament scholar) and Peter Geach (the philosopher). St Deiniol's gradually became known as an attractive retreat for any who wished to study or read or write in peace and quietness with a splendid library always at their disposal. Its fortunes naturally fluctuated. Because of its unique character it was not easy to make its facilities known as widely as they deserved.

I had long since heard of the foundation but I had never visited it until I went for an exploratory weekend, after I had been approached about the editorship of *Theology*. I could see at once that it would be an ideal base for that undertaking. I was very kindly received by the Warden, W. F. Wentworth-Sheilds, who was an unusual kind of man. He had wide interests

St Deiniol's Library, Hawarden

and had had a large experience in Australia, where he had finally been Bishop of Armidale. He was prodigiously modest. It was almost impossible to get him to enter a door before anyone else. If reference was made to the fact of his being a bishop, he would deprecatingly observe that he had been merely a 'bush bishop', as though that were an office in the Church inferior to that of a deacon. He had the rare gift not only of appearing to be interested, but of really being interested, in the concerns of everyone he met. In presiding at meals he would quickly discover what were the predominant interests of those visitors who were sitting next to him and would proceed to develop a conversation on their favourite subjects as though all his life they had been his favourite subjects too. To observe his manners was an education in wardenship.

When he became Warden in 1930 St Deiniol's had been rather run down, but with his arrival it quickly picked up. It was soon so besieged by would-be students of one kind and another, especially undergraduates and clergymen, that a new wing was built on to the hostel which doubled the amount of sleeping accommodation available; and in university vacations often another dozen men had bedrooms in the village while otherwise residing in the hostel.

The bishop-warden's kindness, considerateness and indulgence were balanced by the rigour and severity of the matron, Miss Emberlin, a devoted servant of the foundation, who was known behind her back as 'Miss Ember-days'. She not only managed the Warden, whose health was none too good, with untiring care and skill, but woe betide any luckless visitor who was late for breakfast or who contravened any of her dispositions! I perceived that, should I become Warden, my soul would not be worth calling my own, if she continued as matron. Fortunately no difficulty arose on this score as it was her wish to retire and to keep house for Bishop Wentworth-Sheilds.

However, when I went into residence at the beginning of October 1938, it was by no means a foregone conclusion that I should become Warden. The sub-warden at the time was Dr George Seaver, a man of distinguished mind as readers of his books about Edward Wilson of the Antarctic and about Albert Schweitzer will know; he was also a man of what I can only describe as beautiful character. Like the Warden he excelled in modesty and gentleness. There was nothing of the restless reformer or of the go-getter about him. He would like to have succeeded Wentworth-Sheilds as Warden, but was too diffident to press his candidature strongly. He was a much better man than I in every respect, except perhaps one.

Mark Pattison, in his *Memoirs*, says of himself that he had 'from youth up a restless desire to be always improving himself, other people, all things, all received ways of doing anything'. I know just what he meant and have myself shared that temperamental disease, if it be a disease. In the present case, the consequence was that, when the trustees of St Deiniol's interviewed Seaver and myself, which they did, separately, at a meeting in London in February 1939, he, I imagine, was engagingly inarticulate about what he would do if he were appointed Warden, whereas I submitted ambitious and carefully thought out plans for making St Deiniol's a much more lively centre of thought and influence than it had been heretofore. For good or ill, perhaps with some trepidation, the trustees gave me the appointment.

Dr Seaver, with characteristic generosity, agreed to continue as sub-warden, and he was an ideal colleague, as were also (after he had moved to a parish in 1944) his successors, R. P. McDermott and G. R. Dunstan, and all the other colleagues that I had at St Deiniol's. If the institution prospered, it was the result of team-work, not of individual prowess.

I actually took over the wardenship on 15 July 1939, which meant that I had hardly got into the saddle, as it were, when the Second World War broke out. This might have made, and very nearly did make, havoc of all my hopes and plans. To begin with, a day or two before the declaration of war, when the great but ill-prepared evacuation of our cities was ordained, I received an order to accommodate a hundred blind people from Birkenhead. As the hostel normally held only about thirty people, and as the bedrooms were designed to contain only single beds, this seemed a tall order. The only consolation was that there was no risk of our evacuees wanting to read in the library or of their introducing disorder among the books. Seventy beds were promptly delivered from somewhere, and I well remember fixing them so that there were three or four or even five in a room.

From the outset I was determined, if it was humanly possible and however many evacuees we took in, to keep the library and hostel functioning as usual in spite of war conditions. My belief was – and it was fully justified in the event – that under the pressures, anxieties and harrassing distractions of war there would be plenty of men who would need and want the opportunities for periods of quiet, of thought, and of mental and spiritual refreshment, that St Deiniol's was ideally qualified to provide. Therefore I had no intention of handing over the institution to any government department. Sir Albert Gladstone, who was then the senior trustee, thought I was too sanguine about this. Whatever the circumstances I meant to remain in charge and on the spot. On 2 September I put up a tent (my Fruiting Campaign manse) in the garden, in which I would sleep if there were no room for me in the hostel.

In point of fact when, later on that heavy day, our blind evacuees arrived, there were only eighty of them instead of the expected hundred. So I myself, the sub-warden, the Gladstone research students, and one or two others, could continue to reside in the hostel. I handed over the common room to the blind, and the rest of us retained the use of the dining-room and a small study as a common room. Thanks to the versatility of the domestic staff, we quickly established a new and workable routine.

The incursion of the evacuees indirectly solved one of my most awkward problems. It was a mark of my predecessor's indulgence that he had allowed some elderly (and at this distance of time, one may add, rather odd) men to reside permanently in the hostel. They found it both an agreeable and an economic place in which to live, but it was not what St Deiniol's was intended for. Their presence gave a false impression to visitors and took up room that was required for genuine students. It was the wish of the trustees that I should tackle this problem, and it looked as if it was going to be a ticklish one. I had begun to take steps to persuade these good men to move elsewhere, when the arrival of the evacuees made it imperative that they should leave at once. I am glad to say that they all found satisfactory accommodation elsewhere. Though later in my wardenship I had some curious customers to deal with, I never had this particular problem to solve again.

As regards the blind evacuees, no sooner had the eighty of them settled in than some of them began to yearn for the flesh-pots – or maybe the familiar noises – of Birkenhead. This was of course the period of the phoney war. At the rate of two or three a week they drifted home. Consequently after four or five months only a handful of them remained, and these were transferred to the Old Rectory which until the war had been the Knutsford Test School. Thus St Deiniol's was free to be used again for its proper purposes and, as I had hoped and antici-pated, throughout the war the number of visitors was well maintained.

During 1940, however, another formidable attempt was made to take us over. I looked out of my study window one day and saw advancing down the main drive about half a dozen RAF officers, headed by what must have been at least an Air Vice-Marshal. He informed me that they were proposing to take over the library or part of it as offices for the staff of the Hawarden aerodrome. With as much nonchalance as I could muster I said, 'Let me show you the library', and when inside I added, 'You realize that you will have to find somewhere for these sixty thousand books to be stored safely, as we could not possibly

have them left here, if the library is to be turned into offices.'
Those gallant men were so disconcerted by this unexpected
information that, to my surprise and relief, they went off almost
at once in search of other premises. Though they threatened
that they might return, they never did so and, having with such
ease defeated their machinations, I had confidence that in future
I should be able with equanimity to face the assaults of whole
squadrons of bureaucrats.

I will not say that conditions in St Deiniol's were normal
during the rest of the war. For one thing, both the sub-warden
and I were engaged in civil defence. He was a highly efficient
member of the Observer Corps, and I was an incompetent
Air Raid Warden: one night a week I used to go over the way
and sleep in a stable. There were from time to time battles in
the air in our neighbourhood; we saw in the distance the effects
of the bombing of Liverpool; and Hawarden itself did not escape
damage. The railway station was destroyed by fire.

Then the rationing problems were a constant headache to the
matron and, as we were registered as a catering establishment,
there were many forms to be filled in daily. At the same time,
we were fortunate in having a splendid gardener of the old
school who kept our extensive kitchen gardens in fruitful
production. I myself made a small contribution to food supplies
by starting to keep bees, which I have continued to do ever
since. (At Hawarden I had an apicultural advantage that I have
not had elsewhere; I could transport my hives up the mountains
for the heather harvest each August.) There were times during
the war when we had eight or ten airmen billeted on us, and
we often had groups of chaplains for retreat and conference.

One of the satisfactions enjoyed by a warden of St Deiniol's
is that, within the wide terms of the trust deed and provided
he can commend his projects to the trustees, he has plenty of
scope for initiative. Often in a college or in a parish or in
many other institutions there is an old guard bent on preventing
or obstructing changes or experiments. There was no one at St

Deiniol's sufficiently settled or permanent to constitute an old guard or to impede new developments that might involve a break with tradition. (A break with tradition after my time was the admission of women to stay in the hostel; I should have welcomed it, but the trustees were not yet ready to approve.)

I will mention two or three changes or developments that I was instrumental in introducing. My predecessor had had an elaborate way of observing Founder's Week each year, that is, in addition to Founder's Day which had always been observed. Some eminent divines were invited to give courses of lectures and perhaps as many as a hundred clergymen attended. A huge marquee was put up on the lawn where meals were served. I was myself present on the last of these occasions, two or three weeks before I took over the wardenship. Not only was it a heavy drain on our financial resources which I thought could be better used in getting books for the library, but I became sceptical of the value of the proceedings when one afternoon I was asked to take the chair while Professor C. H. Dodd gave one of his superb lectures on the Fourth Gospel. It was distressing to observe that during the lecture practically the whole auditory fell asleep. I resolved there and then that it was not an exercise that I should be willing to repeat.

In its place the trustees approved of my arranging in the corresponding week each year a conference of about thirty specially invited theologians who discussed a series of learned papers. I remember one year Ronald Gregor Smith, who was a frequent visitor to St Deiniol's and later Primarius Professor of Divinity in Glasgow University, brought Martin Buber to lecture to us. When he appeared it was just as if the prophet Isaiah had come to life again.

Another of my innovations was inviting various groups of people to come and stay in St Deiniol's for periodical weekends (at their own charges), in order to discuss theological, political or social questions. For example, we had a weighty international and ecumenical group that worked for some years on the subject of Natural Law, and eventually published its findings in a small book (*Natural Law: a Christian Reconsideration,* 1946). Another group consisted of Anglican theologians, including Michael Ramsey, F. L. Cross, Austin Farrer and others, who met several times to consider whether there was a case for producing another volume of essays in the *Lux Mundi* tradition. Although we decided in the end against doing so, we found our common deliberations rewarding. A third group consisted of lay people who were within fairly easy reach of Hawarden and who met for three or four weekends a year to discuss a variety of topics of general and personal interest. Among the members of this group I recall especially Professor Lester Smith (at that time Director of Education in Manchester), Mr Walter James (who was then on the staff of the *Manchester Guardian*) and Professor Dorothy Emmet, the philosopher, who (the trustees decreed) had to sleep out but might have meals with the matron and could of course attend our sessions which were held in my study. Then other groups came to Hawarden for which I was not directly responsible, such as the group of dons whose work led after several years' preparation to the writing of Sir Walter Moberly's book *The Crisis in the University* (1949); they held their first two conferences in my study at St Deiniol's, and I wrote one of the series of pamphlets (*Christianity's Need for a Free University,* 1946) which we brought out to open up the subject.

These activities were of course additional to the normal use of the library and hostel by individual students, a term which I use to embrace dons and schoolmasters, general readers and ministers of religion, authors and researchers, as well as undergraduates. Among notable men who stayed with us for considerable periods during or shortly after the war I may mention Dr Thomas Jones (formerly Assistant Secretary of the Cabinet), Professor Karl Mannheim, the sociologist, Dr Georg Misch, the historian of autobiography, Dr Gerhard Leibholz (brother-in-law of Dietrich Bonhoeffer), Dr Hans Ehrenberg, the

Lutheran theologian, D. R. Davies and Hugh Ross Williamson. The two last named stayed at St Deiniol's while they were preparing for ordination in the Church of England. A number of other middle-aged candidates came to us for the same purpose; we did not give them formal lectures, but we guided their reading and were available for consultation at any time. They also made use of our chapel which I brought into full use with a daily round of services.

Attendance at chapel services was of course purely voluntary, but many visitors seemed to appreciate the opportunities that they provided. One evening a week my colleagues or I myself would give an exposition of a passage of Scripture after compline. I laid it down that the passage expounded must be one of the lessons appointed to be read at matins or evensong on the day, so as to prevent our selecting favourite, easy or specially congenial passages. D. R. Davies (who had originally been a miner, then a lion-tamer, then a Nonconformist minister who turned his church into a Labour Church, then after going to Spain for the civil war and after a period of blank despair had experienced a profound re-conversion, as he recorded in his book *On to Orthodoxy*) became so enamoured of the Book of Common Prayer, which was new to him, that he wrote while he was with us that telling book on the General Confession, for which I gave him the gorgeous title *Down Peacock's Feathers* (from the First Book of Homilies). He did not get on with another frequent visitor to St Deiniol's, Robert Sencourt, whose sympathies were with General Franco. One evening after a violent argument in the common room they nearly came to blows and each resorted to me afterwards to have his ruffled feathers smoothed.

One of the merits of St Deiniol's was that it left everyone free to get on with his own work, whether it were reading or writing, without fussing him or expecting him to do anything else, while at the same time any visitor was at liberty to seek the help of any member of the staff if he so desired. Many welcomed the opportunity to meet the many interesting people who came and went, and to talk with them at meals or at other times. On Sunday evenings I used to be 'at home' in my study and somebody who was staying with us would speak on a subject, on which he was specially qualified to speak, with a view to starting a discussion or to provoking questions. For example, Dr Thomas Jones gave a fascinating talk on the diverse ways in which the prime ministers he had served used to prepare their speeches. These discussions went on till 10.30 p.m. or later. In order that we should not go to bed in too serious or agitated a frame of mind I would wind up the proceedings by reading aloud one of Damon Runyon's stories, and I can recommend that prescription as a corporate night-cap.

The amenities offered by St Deiniol's are well enough indicated by the following report which appeared in the *Evening Standard* of 17 March 1944, if you discount what it says about myself:

A man just back from the north of England tells me that he stayed at St Deiniol's Library, at Hawarden, the only residential library in the country. It contains not only the whole of Mr Gladstone's famous library, but 40,000 volumes added since his death, and is still growing.

You can stay for weeks at a time at St Deiniol's, with your own bedroom and study, and have comfortable access to the books. The limited accommodation, I am told, is heavily booked up . . .

The warden himself is one of the most picturesque characters in the Church of England. The Rev. Alec Vidler, bearded and in the early forties, is a wit and a scholar who, in himself, attracts many visitors. He wears the habit of a monk.

Under his presidency the dinner-table conversation is on the same plane as a good High Table at one of the older universities.

Hawarden is in Wales, not in England, and I was at that time a member of the Church in Wales. As for my wearing 'the habit of a monk,' in those days I usually wore indoors a cassock with a scapular (= a glorified apron!). It was about this time that I gave up wearing the so-called clerical collar, which anyhow came into use only in the latter part of the nineteenth century. Before then clerks in holy orders wore a comely white necker-chief or tie. The clerical collar is the least prepossessing form of neckwear that has ever been invented. It was not quite so bad when it was made of linen, but I have to reveal that a great many clerics now wear collars made of plastic or celluloid, such as no self-respecting layman would dream of wearing. Since I adopted a black collar and white tie as the most becom-ing neckwear for the clergy, that is, when they want to wear something distinctive of their profession, I have been glad to see that the idea has caught on in many enlightened circles. A thing that prejudices me against the ordination of women is that they go in for inelegancy of the clerical collar which looks even worse on them than on men.

Another advantage enjoyed by a warden of St Deiniol's is that when he has done all that he ought to do in the administration of the library and hostel and in attending to the needs of visitors he still has plenty of time on his hands. I and my colleagues devoted much care to keeping the flower gardens in attractive condition. I myself made a rather grand rockery and the artist Hugh Buss, who spent a year or more at St Deiniol's and helped with the cataloguing of the library, painted a picture of it with Hawarden church in the background. I still have this picture hung in my bedroom.

But apart from all this I had a lot of time for reading and writing and for what I may call extra-mural activities, which were indeed so varied and extensive that I am going to deal with them in a separate chapter. I did not regard extra-mural activi-ties or writing books as irrelevant to my being Warden, for the more I got about and became known in the academic world, the more I was able to meet potential visitors to the library and expatiate upon its attractions. But before I leave Hawarden for the wider world, there are some further points I want to make.

From what I have said so far it may appear that St Deiniol's was a self-contained and enclosed institution, and so it may have been for temporary visitors. I however made many friends in the village and used to give a certain amount of help to the church. Hawarden is in area a very large parish with six district churches, and although curates were then in good supply some further assistance was often welcomed. I was also a regular attender at the local ministers' fraternal, in which Non-conformists naturally predominated. Sometimes I took a visiting bishop as a guest and observed with amusement how they tumbled over one another in addressing him as 'My Lord'! A Bible study group for the intellectual ladies of Hawarden used to meet in my study, when I expounded a book from the Scriptures to them.

Towards the end of my time at Hawarden the William Temple college, in the foundation of which L. S. Hunter took a leading part, started its life in the Old Rectory and its students of course made much use of our library. They were for the most part women, social or church workers, who took courses in theology and the social sciences. I acted as the first director of studies in theology, and Liverpool University provided sociological teaching. The college did not stay at Hawarden for very long and has gone through various metamorphoses since then.

There was nothing much to be done about party politics during the war, but in the general election of 1945 I did some speaking for Miss Eirene Jones (now Baroness White) who was the Labour candidate for our constituency. Then the clerk to the rural district council and I founded a literary society which met in the council chamber and rapidly acquired popularity. He was secretary and I was chairman. We had a programme of lectures, debates, mock parliaments, and so on.

Finally here, I want to testify to my conviction that no deed of Mr Gladstone's was more inspired that his founding of

St Deiniol's Library. It is the perfect retreat not only for professional students, whether they are old or young, and for men or women who want to write a book in quietude with works of reference at hand and no telephonic or other interruptions, but also for husbands and wives who want a reading 'holiday' whether of a few days' or of longer duration. They are also likely to meet there interesting people from many walks of life and from many parts of the world. It has been disputed whether Mr Gladstone was well-advised to locate this generous foundation at Hawarden. Some would say that it would have been better placed nearer the centre of England where more people would have had easy access to it. It is said that Charles Gore was consulted and urged that it should be in a city rather than in the country. I myself never had any doubt that the founder was right in resisting the advice of those who would have placed it in a great centre of population.

CHAPTER VIII

Extra-mural Activities

—

No hard and fast line can be drawn between my extra-mural and intra-mural activities during my years at Hawarden. While I myself was centred there all the time, many of my employments were circumferenced elsewhere and had no essential connection with St Deiniol's Library. It is about these that I am going to write in this chapter. In some of them I continued to be active after I had left Hawarden and I will round off my account of those while I am on the subject.

I. ST DEINIOL'S KOINONIA

Shortly before the outbreak of war in September 1939 I had decided, with the encouragement of some of my friends, to see whether we could form an unofficial or secret fellowship of youngish Christians who would help one another to work out an authentically Christian understanding of what was taking place in the world and to discover what we ought to be doing about it as members of the Church. We had in mind how in the First World War Christians had often been carried away by tides of emotional and uncritical patriotism: an American author had afterwards written a book with the apposite title, *Preachers Present Arms*. Whether we were priests or laymen, we did not want to repeat that mistake, though most of us were by no means absolute pacifists.

I was well placed to take an initiative in this matter, first because at St Deiniol's I had more time available than most people, and secondly because I had an unusually large acquaintance with young priests, ordinands and laymen who were concerned to bear a faithful witness in the grave events that were coming upon us and that might well disperse us all over the world. The extent of my acquaintance was due, first, to the opportunities I had had during my time at the Oratory House in getting to know a wide range of undergraduates; and, secondly, to the Mission to Oxford University during which I had made many similar contacts there; and thirdly, I would be constantly meeting new visitors to St Deiniol's and ascertaining their dispositions.

So it came about that on 8 September 1939 I sent a confidential circular letter to about fifty of my friends and acquaintances, asking whether they would wish to be kept in touch with one another by correspondence and, when and where possible, by meeting. I enclosed a document in which I tried to adumbrate the theological convictions that we should have in common, our practical objectives, the kinds of reform and renewal in *ecclesia moribunda* for which we should work, and the personal standards of life to which we should aspire. All these would be matters for further consideration and clearer articulation when we could meet, though evidently the outbreak of war was going to make all kinds of meeting more difficult.

The replies I received were not only approving but largely enthusiastic, with the result that from this time onwards I was responsible for sending out circular letters every month or two, which consisted mostly of quotations from letters that had come to me. In April 1940 over twenty of us were able to meet for three days at the Pleshey retreat house in Essex, where the project took firmer shape. The name, 'St Deiniol's Koinonia', requires a little explanation. We intended to eschew all publicity, and succeeded in doing so,[1] but we needed some name

1. Naturally some people beyond our membership heard about it and took an interest in it. It may be that, because of my part in it, William Temple, when Archbishop of Canterbury, asked me to go and see him at Lambeth, since he was concerned about the apparent gulf between younger and older theologians.

by which we ourselves could refer to our undertaking and, as I was to act as secretary and was located at St Deiniol's, that seemed a suitable place-name. Members were of course encouraged to visit Hawarden, and many did so at one time or another. The New Testament Greek word, *koinonia*, which is usually translated 'fellowship' (for example, in Acts ii. 42; II Cor. xiii. 13) but is much richer in meaning than any single English word can show, was becoming something of a vogue word and deservedly so: its wealth of significance was about to be brought out in L. S. Thornton's book, *The Common Life in the Body of Christ* (1941).

It would be invidious to name any of the fifty or so members of St Deiniol's Koinonia who are still alive (as most of them happily are). A considerable proportion of them were to become well-known when they were older. I will name only those who are no longer alive: D. R. Davies (see p. 103), Gilbert Hort (grandson of F. J. A. Hort, who had great potentialities as a theologian but who died prematurely when serving with the Cambridge Mission to Delhi), F. E. Lunt (later Bishop of Stepney), Richard Inge (W. R. Inge's son, who was killed in the war), Denys Munby (the Oxford economist), Alan Richardson (later Dean of York), and Algy Robertson (see p. 35).

Some members were able to form Christian cells in their own localities, and I was able to send out information about these and other enterprises in my circular letters. These letters also contained frank and often provocative statements of opinion about questions that were exercising our minds and were under discussion among us: statements that were not ripe for publication, but that contributed to a continuing and lively interchange of thought. Although the war prevented us from holding many meetings, the circulation of correspondence was found to be so useful by the members that I continued with it not only after the war but after I left Hawarden when it became known as 'the Windsor Correspondence', and later as 'the Cambridge Correspondence', and finally as 'the Woolwich

Correspondence' when Dr John Robinson kindly took over responsibility for it.

The ideas that were canvassed in our letters might seem unexciting now but at the time they would have been regarded as radical, if not as heretical, though not as progressive, for none of us were credulous about secular progress or entertained Utopian expectations. I will not say more about them here, since similar ideas were naturally handled, if more judiciously, in *Theology* and in other publications that I shall be mentioning.

2. EDITING *Theology*

I have already explained the circumstances in which I undertook the editorship of the monthly journal, *Theology*. During the next twenty-five years (that is, from 1939 to 1964) it was one of my principal employments, though it did not take up so much of my time as many people supposed, partly because throughout this period I had secretarial help of one kind or another, and also because the business-like habits that I had acquired during my year with Vidler and Sons Ltd stood me in good stead.

When I became Warden of St Deiniol's it was agreed that I would engage the services of a secretary so long as I continued to edit *Theology*. At first I had a lay secretary, but I found that it would be more serviceable if I had someone in holy orders who could help in a general way with my duties at St Deiniol's, and I was fortunate in persuading two of my friends, first, John Nias, and then, Wilfrid Browning, to help in this way. They spent their weekends at a nautical training school at Heswall on Wirral to which they became chaplains but during the week were very welcome members of the staff of St Deiniol's.

It had been my intention from the outset to broaden the basis on which *Theology* was edited so as to extend its appeal and so as to make it an organ of Anglican theological thought as a whole and not only of Cambridge liberal Catholicism. I therefore formed a small advisory committee of which the original members were: F. A. Cockin, L. J. Collins, F. L. Cross, Norman Sykes, and Ashley Sampson. They not only met with me at fairly regular intervals but also in my early days were good enough to comment on the drafts of my editorials and to come up with a variety of suggestions. In addition, I wrote to a large number of theologians, representative of different schools of thought in the Church of England, and to Christian men of letters, explaining my editorial aims and asking them to allow their names to appear as 'collaborators', which would mean that they would assist me from time to time with advice about manuscripts that were submitted and other matters and would be willing to do some reviewing. Nearly all those whom I invited readily agreed: the only ones who refused or who were dubious were some Anglo-Catholics, such as Will Spens, who did not approve of my casting my net so wide or of the company I seemed likely to be keeping! Among the laymen who agreed to collaborate were: Montgomery Belgion, T. S. R. Boase, T. S. Eliot, C. S. Lewis, J. Middleton Murry, Joseph Needham, and Charles Williams.

I made no attempt to conceal the fact that I was initiating a change of editorial policy which incidentally was symbolized by a change in the format and cover which had previously been a dull grey but now blossomed forth in bright primrose! We lost a few elderly readers who complained that *Theology* now looked like a French novel!

In my first editorial (January 1939) I stated what were my three aims:

(a) to provide a medium through which all that is best in contemporary theology may reach the clergy, the laity, and those outside the Church who are looking towards Christianity for a reasonable and relevant faith;

(b) to serve as an organ where Anglican writers with different associations and various special interests may meet and contribute to the clarification and exposition of the faith which has their allegiance;

(c) to serve as a liaison between theological thought and those movements in contemporary literature, art and political philosophy which are working towards a re-discovery of the significance of the Christian tradition.

Just as it is an advantage to the new vicar of a parish if his predecessor has more or less emptied the church or let it run badly down, so it was an advantage to me that it was fairly easy to make *Theology* more readable and interesting than it had been recently, and I was of course fortunate in securing the support and co-operation of so strong and varied a body of collaborators. On the other hand, during the war which was soon upon us, paper rationing and other things were to restrict expansion of the size of the journal and of its circulation. When I took over the circulation was between seventeen and eighteen hundred. Quite speedily we increased it by thirty per cent, and in the course of time and when conditions permitted, we worked it up to over five thousand, which I reckoned was about right if we were not to lower our sights.

My predecessors had left the editorial secretary of SPCK, Dr Lowther Clarke (whose services to *Theology* were incalculable), to arrange for the reviewing of books, but I decided to take this over myself and devoted a good deal of care to it. In particular, I made it my business to collect from my collaborators and others the names of young and as yet untried scholars together with information about their special interests so that I could build up a fresh team of reviewers. This proved very rewarding, and I still have the satisfaction of meeting from time to time well-known authorities on this or that who tell me that it was I who first gave them an opportunity of reviewing books. I also took trouble over the selection of correspondence for publication, of which I always received a lot more than I could publish. This was a healthy sign. Readers often told me that the first thing that they looked at when a new issue arrived was the 'Letters to the Editor'.

The only other thing I need record about my editorship of *Theology* (the volumes of which are available for inspection by anyone who wants to go further into the matter) is the attempt that was made to curtail my freedom, if not to get me sacked. It was the outcome of the editorial that I wrote at the outbreak of the war for the October 1939 issue. This opened with a quotation from Reinhold Niebuhr's *Reflections on the End of an Era* and was designed to be a warning against any facile simplification or moralizing of the issues involved in the war. It contained passages such as the following:

> We are all caught in the meshes of a situation in which no course of action is innocent, yet in which we must needs choose some course of action. An Englishman cannot fail to recognize the depth and sincerity of the conviction that the forcible overthrow of Nazi principles is a moral duty which is laid upon this country. But for our part we cannot repeat the national slogan that 'our conscience is clear' ... The devilry of Hitlerism does not automatically transform us into angels of light or prophets of the Lord . . . International politics are, in fact, a struggle for power which can be only partially and precariously moralized.
>
> It is the duty of the Church to insist upon this unpalatable truth. The Church best serves the nation not by uncritically endorsing the pure idealism of its professed war aims, but by proclaiming the Word of God, which shows even the noblest human purposes to be shot through with sin. The Church best serves the nation not by seeking to keep up the nation's morale, but by humbling its pride . . .

I was at the same time engaged in enlarging on this theme in a book entitled *God's Judgment on Europe* (1940) which Longmans had asked me to write.

It was only after an interval of about six months that Dr

Lowther Clarke, as editorial secretary of SPCK, told me that their literature committee, which had an oversight of their publications, was agitated about my October 1939 editorial. This was at the time of the fall of France. He wrote to me on 1 June 1940:

> The outlook is so serious that the less we argue the better it will be for all. Quite possibly we shall have to close down *Theology*. But we cannot permit anything to be published which can be interpreted as anti-British propaganda or as tending to weaken the national will for victory. We happen to know that, as a result of the October editorial, *Theology* is one of a number of papers which are being closely watched. To have it suspended by Government would be a blow, perhaps a mortal one, to SPCK.
>
> You may think this deplorable, and that we ought to stand firm for Christian liberty, but if you are wise you will accept *force majeure*.
>
> As to immediate action, I must closely scan the proofs and hold back for discussion with you anything I think risky.

I made it clear that while I was at any time willing to consider any questions he cared to raise at the proof stage, especially about matters that might affect the reputation of SPCK, I was not prepared to be told what I might or might not say about the war and issues of that kind.

After some further correspondence I wrote to him on 27 June 1940:

> With regard to *Theology*. I agree that it would be best to proceed, and if any concrete issue is raised by your Committee I can then consider the matter, as, indeed, I should have been willing to do at any time in the past . . .
>
> I don't think it will be profitable at present to pursue a discussion about the October editorial. I need only say that I neither withdraw nor regret any of it.

Lowther Clarke, who at first seemed to have been rattled like many other people at that time, soon took a calmer view, and indeed stood by me. The agitation had been started by a member of his committee who had proposed that they should seek a new editor, but his proposal had not been seconded. I discovered his identity only later: it was Dr X, who during the 1930s had shown a compromising sympathy for the Nazi movement and was now no doubt anxious by an excess of patriotism to cause that to be forgotten. My position as editor was never again seriously threatened, though there were some rumblings in 1951 when I published a well-informed article by Walton Hannah, entitled 'Should a Christian be a Freemason?' He answered the question in the negative and stirred up some rather hysterical correspondence. The Archbishop of Canterbury (Fisher) called for a report on the matter. I was then at Windsor and King George VI asked to see a copy of the article, but he did not take it amiss. The literature committee of SPCK were naturally reluctant to get rid of me while the journal was becoming increasingly successful by attracting a growing proportion of young and lay readers.

3. THE MOOT

In July 1937 there had been held at Oxford an ecumenical conference on 'Church, Community and State' attended by over four hundred delegates from forty different countries, though none were allowed to come from Germany. The secretary and chief organizer of the conference was Dr J. H. Oldham, a layman who was already well-known because of his services to the missionary movement and his book, *Christianity and the Race Problem* (1924). He had seen to it that the preparatory work for the conference was done by real experts in the various subjects that were to be considered; he had grasped the vitally important point that Christian social witness should mean lay people in positions of responsibility *doing* things, and not merely clerics and ecclesiastical assemblies *saying* things; and it was his intention that the conference should be followed up in as realistic a way as possible. In three of the undertakings that he set on foot I was to become involved.

It had been borne in upon him that, whereas the fascists and the communists, who with their totalitarian regimes were setting the pace in social change and in international relations, had or appeared to have definite creeds of ideologies that engaged the passionate allegiance of whole nations and the active sympathy of fellow-travellers elsewhere, the so-called western democracies had no firm alternative faith or at least were vague and inarticulate about what they really stood for. So far as Britain was concerned it seemed to Oldham that there was an urgent need to promote the exploration and articulation of a basic social faith to which the British people could feel they were dedicated and which was their constructive alternative to totalitarianism. This faith could not be a simple affirmation of Christianity, since, on the one hand, only a minority of people in Britain were convinced Christians or likely to become so in the proximate future and, on the other hand, Christians themselves were by no means agreed on the implications of their creed. Oldham therefore decided to try to draw together a small group of thinkers with varied background, experience and expertise, who would undertake to think this matter through. He used to say that what was needed was a group like the Utilitarians early in the nineteenth century who would work out and disseminate a social philosophy appropriate to our time as they did to theirs.

Oldham ('Joe' to his friends) was a Scot and an extraordinary man, though he did not look it. Short in stature, somewhat frail in physique, and handicapped by deafness which was not much relieved by the hearing aids he used, he had a rare gift for getting on to speaking terms with intellectuals and men of affairs of many sorts and of securing their interest in the ideas he propounded and also of engaging their affections. I would not say that he himself was an originating thinker, but he had a tireless capacity for listening and for picking other people's brains, and above all for bringing together men and women who normally would never meet but who could fruitfully stimulate and fertilize one another's minds.

The group of a dozen or fifteen people which he constituted in 1938 and which was known to its members as 'The Moot' was of this kind. Its proceedings were entirely private and its existence was known to very few people. If it exerted influence, it was by its effects on the thinking and writings and actions of its members, not by issuing any statements as a group. Very little has so far been published about it, but Roger Kojecky's *T. S. Eliot's Social Criticism* (1971) contains reliable information as well as a list of the regular members and of others who were present at some of the meetings. The regular members included John Baillie (the Scottish theologian), Sir Fred Clarke (the educationalist), T. S. Eliot, Sir Hector Hetherington (Principal of Glasgow University), Professor H. A. Hodges (the philosopher), Karl Mannheim (the sociologist), Sir Walter Moberly (then chairman of the University Grants Committee), and John Middleton Murry. Christopher Dawson and Adolf Löwe were members until they left for the USA. For some reason which I have never understood, I was asked to be a member and I was able to attend regularly.

The Moot met for about four long weekends each year, usually in the country and finally at St Julian's in Sussex. For each meeting some members prepared papers for discussion. It was a Christian gathering and there were daily periods of prayer, though some members were would-be rather than professing Christian believers. Eric Fenn, who was a regular member, acted as scribe and produced invaluable summaries of our discussions which were afterwards duplicated and circulated to the members. A considerable proportion of the papers prepared for the Moot, when revised in the light of discussion, found their way into print whether in periodicals or books.

Hardly any of the regular members are still alive but I think they would all testify that they learned an immense amount through the Moot, not least from those members who started with presuppositions far removed from their own. For instance, I was constantly struck by the sympathy that grew up between T. S. Eliot and Karl Mannheim and by the way they impressed and influenced each other. In some respects Mannheim was the central figure in the Moot. His conception of 'planning for freedom' as the proper alternative to totalitarianism, on the one hand, and to British *laissez faire* or muddling through, on the other, was one that commended itself to us. It could be said that we were engaged in exploring the philosophical, ethical, sociological, political, theological, and indeed all other aspects of it. The centrality of Mannheim's role is shown by the fact that, when he died suddenly in 1947, we spontaneously stopped meeting; at any rate Oldham never called us together again.

Though I, along with Middleton Murry, took a less sanguine or more gloomy view than most of the members about the possibility of preventing the final collapse or disintegration of our western technological civilization, Mannheim persuaded me that so long as there is any opening whatever for working for the kind of free society that he envisaged one was morally bound to do so. It was with that impulsion that I took part in two other outcomes of the 1937 Oxford Conference that Dr Oldham initiated and that I have yet to describe, namely the *Christian News-Letter* and the Christian Frontier Council. My connection with the latter belongs to my next chapter. I also learned a lot from Oldham's conduct of the Moot about how to constitute and chair similar groups at Hawarden and elsewhere.

4. THE CHRISTIAN NEWS-LETTER

When war broke out in September 1939, Dr Oldham, prompted

by Miss Eleanora Iredale who had been working with him and was skilled in administration and in raising funds, undertook to edit a news-letter, which would resemble the then familiar *National News-Letter* of Stephen King-Hall, but would look at what was happening from a Christian point of view and would seek to cast light on the many dark and deep questions that were baffling thoughtful people. It was to be a co-operative enterprise and Oldham was able to give the names of about fifty people who had promised to assist him. Each issue contained a letter from the editor, some news and notes, and a supplement that dealt at more length with some burning question or current topic of importance.

The *Christian News-Letter* quickly caught on and very soon had a circulation of over ten thousand. It evidently met a need that was widely felt. In the first issue (18 October 1939) Oldham mentioned that a list of subscribers would be kept in two different places in case the London office was destroyed by a bomb, and that I would be associated with him in the editorial work. As I lived at Hawarden it was improbable that we should both be knocked out in the same air raid!

Such help as I was able to give consisted, first, in travelling regularly to London for the meetings of a small editorial board (of which T. S. Eliot, Lord Hambleden and Philip Mairet were other members) that carefully scrutinized and commented on the matter that was being prepared for the next issue. Secondly, later on I became responsible for a few issues when Oldham needed a holiday and I occasionally contributed a supplement to the *Christian News-Letter*. Thirdly, I undertook to be general editor of a series of small books (The *Christian News-Letter* Books) to be published by the Sheldon Press, which would be designed to provide a fuller treatment of some of the subjects that were being ventilated in the *Christian News-Letter* itself. The first batch of these books, which was ready in March 1940, included *The Resurrection of Christendom* by Oldham himself, *Europe in Travail* by Middleton Murry, and *Christianity and Justice* by O. C. Quick. Among later books in the series were: Karl Barth's *A Letter to Great Britain from Switzerland*, E. G. Rupp's *Is this a Christian Country?*, George Every's *Christian Discrimination*, Adolf Löwe's *The Universities in Transformation*, and Eric Gill's *Christianity and the Machine Age*.

When the blitz came upon us, the *Christian News-Letter* office had to be moved for a time to Manchester College, Oxford, and the editorial board met there. I remember spending a night with C. S. Lewis in Magdalen College, and another in the President's Lodgings at Corpus Christi College where Eliot was in the next bedroom to mine; soon after we had retired, there was a general commotion as a hot-water bottle had burst in his bed! But often I travelled to London or Oxford from North Wales by the night train. There is no doubt from the large correspondence we received that the *Christian News-Letter* was greatly appreciated in the war years by a wide variety of people. It distilled in short compass the results of a lot of hard thinking, some of which was generated behind the scenes in the Moot.

5. MISCELLANEOUS WRITINGS

Conditions could not have been more favourable than they were at St Deiniol's Library both for occasional writing and for the composition of books. During my time there I contributed more articles and book reviews to weekly papers, religious and secular, than I have done, or have wanted to do, since. I also broadcast some talks that appeared in *The Listener*. As regards the religious press, while from time to time I wrote for *The Guardian*, *The Church of England Newspaper*, *The British Weekly*, and *The Record*, I contributed most often to *The Church Times* for which I was regularly asked to review books, write leading articles and other features (all unsigned, as was the practice then and one that I prefer). While this may have been a useful, as well as a remunerative, experience, I was not sorry when *The Church Times* dropped me without explanation, for I had never been entirely happy with its tone or standpoint. Perhaps that was the explanation!

As regards books, nearly all my compositions have resulted from invitations to give courses of academic lectures, or to conduct university missions, or from similar requests. Of the six books that I published while I was at Hawarden, I will say rather more about the first two – *God's Judgment on Europe* (1940) and *Secular Despair and Christian Faith* (1941) – than about the others, not because they were more important, but because they provide an occasion to say something about a supposed change in my outlook or in my theological stance. I can best introduce the matter by citing a review in *The British Weekly* (26 June 1941) by Dr John McConnachie. He wrote:

> Alec R. Vidler has been swept from the calmer waters of his previous book, *A Plain Man's Guide to Christianity,* into a vortex of tense feeling to which he gives utterance in *Secular Despair and Christian Faith* . . .
>
> We are living, he holds, in the last stages of an epoch which began at the Renaissance, since when man has been engaged in a tremendous secular experiment, which has turned to his own destruction. And now there is no hope for him, unless he is driven to complete despair, not of God or of the Universe, but of himself, and the only answer to this despair is to be found in the Christian Faith. The 'grand English heresy' of salvation by decency must be replaced by the fundamental Christian doctrine of justification by faith, which modern English Christianity has eviscerated. How this doctrine puts all our activities – marriage – the family – politics – in a new light, and provides them with a new dynamic he goes on to show.

The book he was reviewing reproduced verbatim the addresses

that I had given during a mission to Liverpool University in February 1941. I took part in similar missions to a number of universities during this period: Leeds (1943), Trinity College, Dublin (1944), Cambridge (1947), and Edinburgh (1948). In Leeds and Dublin my fellow missioner was Alexander Miller, for whom I had a warm admiration. He was a New Zealander who had joined the Iona Community. His early death was a serious loss to the Christian cause. We had both been deeply influenced by the Christian realism of Reinhold Niebuhr and saw eye to eye about most things.

I myself had been what is nowadays called a 'doom-watcher' since the 1920s. That is to say, I had felt sure that we were living in the autumn or fall of a civilization, though it was not possible to say how protracted its last phases would be or what form its final collapse would take. The onset of the Second World War naturally enforced this sense of impending doom, as have many subsequent events. In seeking to interpret what was happening I was influenced not only by Niebuhr, but by D. R. Davies, himself an ardent Niebuhrian, and Hans Ehrenberg, with both of whom I consorted much at Hawarden. Ehrenberg was a learned German pastor with a sense of humour, who had got to Britain after being in a concentration camp. He impelled me to reckon with the person and teaching of Martin Luther, and in particular brought home to me how cardinal and far-reaching is the Pauline doctrine of justification by faith, *sola gratia, sola fide*. While of course I read the so-called 'crisis' theologians, Karl Barth and Emil Brunner, they did not make the same impact on my mind as did the early twentieth-century British theologian, P. T. Forsyth, who, Barth's son Marcus justly observed, was our forerunner of his father.

The consequence of all this, and of other influences that I have already indicated, was that my message at this time (as evidenced by the two books of which I am now speaking) was often characterized as a 'gospel of despair'. I used to say that Christianity had first to be presented and accepted as bad news

123

before it could be heard as good news, and that only when men had been driven to despair of their capacity to put themselves or the world to rights would they move into the area where they could take in the marvellous truth that we are put right not by anything we can do ourselves but by what God has already done for us in Christ.

Perhaps I can best illustrate my new emphasis by explaining in what sense I now used the word 'liberalism'. It is a word that has had many connotations, good, bad, and indifferent. Following Niebuhr, I used it now, as I said in *God's Judgment on Europe* (p. 15), 'as a portmanteau term for the body of ideas and for the *Weltanschauung* which came to exercise a dominant influence in European culture during the eighteenth and nineteenth centuries and the development of which can be traced back to the Renaissance.' A little later in my C. J. Cadoux lecture of 1951 I quoted a Belgian jesuit's description of liberalism in theology as he knew it on the continent. It is a description that hits the mark:

They spoke no longer of redemption but of civilization; no longer of salvation but of culture; no longer of sin but ignorance; no longer of heaven but of progress; no longer of the Church but of humanity; no longer of the Creed but of Science; no longer of eternity but of the future . . . One no longer discussed miracle, one passed over it, as one passed over the Old Testament, the obscure promises to the Jews, and nine-tenths of the Gospel. Suffering was only a false note. One contrived to reduce it, or – who knows? – perhaps one day to eliminate it scientifically. Man was no longer for himself a tragedy; and God having ceased to be embarrassing was no more than a majestic decoration. The whole nineteenth century lived with this idea – however preposterous it seems – that man was going by his own efforts alone to make the earth a heaven and himself an embodiment of wisdom (see my *Essays in Liberality*, p. 16).

'Secular humanism' is probably a better term for this way of thinking. However much I attacked and denounced liberalism if defined in this way, I never abandoned, and trust that I never shall abandon, my attachment to the virtues, the temper, and the cast of mind for which I would use the epithet 'liberal' with 'liberality' as its substantive. 'Here,' I said in the same lecture, 'the word "liberal" denotes not a creed or a set of philosophical assumptions or any 'ism, but a frame of mind, a quality of character, which it is easier no doubt to discern than to define. A liberal-minded man is free from narrow prejudice, generous in his judgment of others, open-minded, especially to the reception of new ideas or proposals for reform. Liberal is the opposite not of conservative, but of fanatical or bigoted or intransigent. It points to the *esprit large* and away from the *idée fixe*.'

My friend and former mentor Wilfred Knox did not at first appreciate this distinction and was distressed by my new theological orientation and by what he looked upon as my flirtation with what was then known as 'neo-orthodoxy'. But this was mainly a misunderstanding and later, when he had read Niebuhr's Gifford lectures on *The Nature and Destiny of Man*, he wrote and told me what a great work he considered that to be. I do not deny that at the time of which I am speaking I overstated 'the gospel of despair' or got it out of proportion. Charles Raven in his book *Good News of God* and elsewhere used somewhat violently to attack this way of presenting the gospel and indeed anything in which he could detect the influence of Reinhold Niebuhr or of 'the theology of crisis' which he regarded as pathological.

Michael Ramsey, reviewing my book in *Theology*, was more temperate in criticism and I should now accept what he said:

My criticism is not of the austerity of the theme, but of the emphasis on 'despair' as a necessary stage in the turning of men to God . . . Assuredly the New Testament shows the necessity for all of a shattering of pride and a conviction of sin and failure. But I cannot find in the New Testament any evidence that 'despair' or 'bad news' is a necessary or normal part of the process.

Before I leave the subject, I would add that I concur with the confession that Reinhold Niebuhr himself made towards the end of his life (in 1960):

> When I find neo-orthodoxy turning into sterile orthodoxy or a new Scholasticism, I find that I am a liberal at heart, and that many of my broadsides at liberalism were indiscriminate.

My other books written during this period I can mention more briefly. In 1943 Dr Fisher, Bishop of London, invited me to write his Lenten book for the following year. I had material for it available in a course of addresses that I had given in Holy Week at St John's Kirk, Perth. Incidentally, by preaching in the established Church of Scotland I had incurred the grave displeasure of the episcopalian Bishop of St Andrews, who was a convert from presbyterianism. He had tried unsuccessfully to get both the Bishop of St Asaph, in whose diocese Hawarden was situated, and the Archbishop of Canterbury (Temple) to prevent or dissuade me from my purpose.

I had met Dr Fisher, when he was Bishop of Chester. Lady Gladstone had invited us to dinner together. Then, after he was translated to London, I had conducted one of his ordination retreats at Fulham Palace during the height of the blitz. I remember that Malcolm Muggeridge, who was then in the army and whom I was seldom able to meet during the war, came to dine with us one evening, and that the bishop's chaplain (F. C. Synge) and I slept on the ground floor in the library while the bishop descended through a trap door into a cellar or basement beneath.

I introduced my book, which was entitled *Christ's Strange*

Work, by saying, 'I have not to apologize for adding to the books on a well-worn theme, since heretofore, so far as I have been able to discover, not only has the title of this book been unused, but no English writer has dealt with its central subject, namely, the three uses of God's Law.' This is the only one of my theological writings about which I am still a little vain and to the theme of which I attach as much importance now as I did in 1944. However, instead of blowing my own trumpet, I will let Dr Alan Richardson do so for me. He wrote to me at the time from Durham:

> I do not usually buy or read Lenten books, but I did this year, and I am writing to say how much benefit I derived from doing so. It is a long time since I read so small a book which dealt so very adequately with so new and so important a subject. What a lot of sloppy thinking we were all guilty of in the years before 1939 on this theme of Law, State and Order. I am glad that there is now a book to which one can direct people on this matter and that it is so good a book as *Christ's Strange Work.*

A revised edition, with additional material, was published in 1963.

In 1941 I was invited to deliver a course of four lectures at University College, Bangor, on 'Christianity and Statesmanship'. During my visit I was accommodated at an hotel at which Wee Georgie Wood was also staying in order to do some broadcasts for the BBC. In view of my position at Hawarden it was natural that I connected the subject of my lectures with Mr Gladstone, and I read for the first time his early work on *The State in its relations with the Church* which had for long been disregarded because of the way Macaulay had handled it and because of Gladstone's own subsequent abandonment of his theory. But it seemed to me to raise many interesting, living, and important questions, and so after my visit to Bangor I did much further work on the subject from which there emerged in 1945 my book *The Orb and the Cross: a normative study in the relations of Church and State with reference to Gladstone's early writings.*

It produced a lot of long and mostly appreciative reviews which gave me plenty of food for further thought on what Dr Kitson Clark, in his review, justly called 'an old, insoluble, but still urgent problem'. I have from time to time returned to the question of Church-State relations, but I did not pursue my Gladstonian studies any further. I will confess that I have sometimes lamented that a sense of piety did not direct me to the study of Disraeli rather than of Gladstone, since the former's literary style is much more scintillating. *The Orb and the Cross,* like some of my other early books, was disfigured by being overloaded with footnotes, a fault that I have since sought to correct.

I presume that it was with regard to the books that I had so far written that in June 1946 to my surprise I was made an honorary Doctor of Divinity of the University of Edinburgh, an honour that I had had no reason to anticipate. What was still more surprising was that, when I went to Edinburgh for the degree ceremony, the university spokesman who cited my credentials said, among other things, that I had taken 'a responsible concern in a remote missionary field as a Commissioner for New Guinea'. I had never been within thousands of miles of New Guinea! What had happened was that an entry under my name in *Crockford's Clerical Directory* 'Commiss. New Guinea, from 1936' had been taken to mean that I had been a District Commissioner in New Guinea during the war when the country had been overrun by the Japanese, whereas it really meant that I had been asked by the Bishop of New Guinea (my old friend, Philip Strong) to act as one of his Commissaries in England, that is, to interview on his behalf volunteers for missionary service and to serve on the home committee of the mission.

It will be convenient to mention the last two books that

I wrote at Hawarden in connection with my first visit to America.

6. FIRST VISIT TO AMERICA

I have plenty of detailed information about the three months that I spent in America in the autumn of 1947, because in 1946 I had resumed, after an interval of about twenty-five years, the practice of keeping a daily journal which I have continued ever since. But I have never cared for reading travel books or travel diaries, so I am not going to inflict one on anybody now. My visit to the USA originated in an invitation to deliver the Hale lectures at the Seabury-Western Seminary, Evanston, Illinois. The Dean there kindly offered to arrange an extensive lecturing and preaching tour for me. I went to many places in New England and also had engagements in Washington and Chicago, and I was able to stay for a time with relatives in Canada.

I saw a good deal of the Niebuhrs, and met W. H. Auden in their apartment in New York. I had previously met him many years before when he had accompanied his mother, who was a keen Anglo-Catholic, to a party in St Aidan's parish, Birmingham. I noted on the present occasion that he said he was very fond of Disraeli's novels and spoke of Dizzy's play in blank verse which opens with high mass being celebrated at three altars concurrently in Seville cathedral. I was familiar with the novels, but had never heard of the play. Of course I met a great many people and received generous hospitality as I travelled around, but the only other notable I will mention is Professor A. N. Whitehead, to whom Professor Dorothy Emmet had given me an introduction. I called on him and his wife on 3 December 1947 which was less than a month before his death. He was 86 but apart from deafness seemed to be in good condition. Mrs Whitehead said that she had never been more proud of being British than when at the end of the war

Britain turned down Churchill as a peace-time minister, since that showed wonderful political wisdom.

My Hale Lectures were on the theology of Frederick Denison Maurice and were published with that title in England, but in the USA with the title *Witness to the Light*. I had for long wanted to study Maurice's thought, and I certainly found that for me he was a seminal theologian. Most people, who had heard of him, supposed him to have been an early Christian socialist, which was quite misleading, since his socialism was of a very peculiar and dubious kind, and anyhow he was first and last a theologian. My book, *The Theology of F. D. Maurice* (1948), was designed to introduce him in that character and to illustrate with copious quotation the main elements in his teaching. Since then, a considerable literature about him has grown up.

Studying Maurice had a marked effect on my thinking, and as an appendage to this book I will mention my smaller work, *Good News for Mankind* (1947), which consisted of the addresses that I had given during the mission to Cambridge University earlier in that year. This book bears unmistakable evidence, even in its title, of the influence of Maurice's teaching. He had criticized many of the theologians of his own day on the ground that they made 'the sinful man and not the God of all grace the foundation of Christian Theology'. I realized that that is what I had been doing in my earlier mission addresses on 'secular despair', when I was too much under the spell of my eloquent friend D. R. Davies, who had been practically obsessed with the primacy of the doctrine of original sin. At Cambridge I struck a much more positive note, and my addresses there won the warm approbation of Charles Raven, who had so much deplored my previous utterances. He even urged me to be a candidate for a Cambridge professorship that was vacant at the time!

I was vexed that, when *Good News for Mankind* appeared in print, a tiresome error had made its way on to the first page after I had passed the proofs. My visit to Cambridge had also met with adverse conditions, for, on the one hand, there was a heavy fall of snow during the week of the mission and, on the other hand, I was afflicted by a severe attack of laryngitis. If I was able to retain any voice at all, it was because my fellow Oratorian, Christopher Waddams, Tutor of St Catharine's College, with whom I stayed, got his medical adviser to supply a potent drug for me to inhale. Some years later I took part in a mission to Durham University and my addresses there will have been much more an echo of *Good News for Mankind* than of *Secular Despair and Christian Faith*.

CHAPTER IX

Windsor and 'The Doves'

I had no wish to move from Hawarden and should have been glad to continue as Warden of St Deiniol's Library until I retired. I could think of no more agreeable position in which to spend the rest of my working days, and I used to hope that, when I retired, I might have a cottage in the village from which I should still be able to make use of the library. However, while I have not been ambitious for moves or for what is called promotion, it is probably a good thing that circumstances have not allowed me to stay too long in any one employment, in which I might easily have settled down too comfortably or become stale.

In the summer of 1946 a proposal had been made through the agency of J. H. Oldham and others that Lesslie Newbigin and I should become joint-secretaries of the British Council of Churches (BCC) which they wanted to see playing a more imaginative, and less purely bureaucratic, part in the ecumenical movement and on behalf of the churches in Britain. Newbigin's work in South India and as a theologian is well-known: there is no one with whom I should have been happier to work. He was in England at the time and we were able to meet and consider the matter. But neither of us felt called to give up what we were doing for an office job in London, whatever possibilities it may have had. I myself wrote to Oldham as follows (30 June 1946):

> If what you want are secretaries who will take over the London office . . . and begin by carrying on the whole

show as it is at present though with the possibility of much subsequent transformation, then I must say not only that I do not feel called to it, but that I feel called not to do it.

On the other hand, which seems very unlikely, if the BCC were contemplating a fresh set up which no doubt would have to include a London office and some of the machinery that is at present centred there, but which had as the centre of its life and activities a sort of ecumenical centre in the country . . . where there would be a group of people living and thinking, praying and worshipping, together – where both groups and individuals could come and stay – from which it was hoped that the ecumenical understanding and spirit would grow and radiate, perhaps leading to the setting up of similar centres elsewhere in the country – well then, *if* this were being seriously contemplated, I should feel very differently about any call that was made on me . . . But I fear it is so improbable that a transformation would be effected at the outset that it is not worth my saying any more about it . . .

While I was given to understand that those concerned had a good deal of sympathy with my idea, it was deemed to be quite impracticable, and so that was that.

It was in August 1948 that I received an invitation to become a canon of St George's Chapel, Windsor. The King's invitation came to me in the first instance not from Downing Street but through the Dean of Windsor (Bishop Eric Hamilton); the prime minister wrote to me only at a later stage, since his part in nominations to Windsor canonries was purely formal. I am not sure exactly how the invitation was contrived, but members of the Christian Frontier Council certainly had something to do with it, and I must now explain what that was and why its members should have taken an interest in my future.

The Christian Frontier Council (CFC) was another prong, so to speak, in Oldham's follow-up of the Oxford Conference of

1937. Though I knew about it, I had nothing directly to do with it until 1948. It was an association of Christian lay men and women who held responsible positions in public life. It included, for example, ministers in both labour and conservative governments, industrialists, educationalists, scientists, etc., etc. They were not a company of intellectuals like the Moot, though naturally they all had good minds and were concerned to work out what bearing their faith as Christians had, or ought to have, on their official responsibilities and on all kinds of social tasks. They were very busy people and needed to be serviced by someone who had the time to get to know them personally, to make arrangements for their meetings, and to superintend all the secretarial work involved. I shall say more later about the activities and ramifications of the CFC.

It had hitherto been served by the same staff and office as the *Christian News-Letter*, headed by Dr Oldham and Mrs Kathleen Bliss who had taken over the editorship of the *Christian News-Letter*. Dr Oldham himself had now retired, though like the high priest Annas in the gospels he remained an influential figure behind the scenes. If the work of the CFC was to be carried on, it was essential that someone else should be found to undertake responsibility for it.

While I felt no special competence for this undertaking, I regarded it as a task of great importance, and if others deemed me suited for it, it had a strong call upon me. For instance, one member of the Council wrote to me as follows in July 1948:

> I have longed for some way to be found for getting you into a central position for helping us laymen to see what we ought to do within the total strategy of the Church, how we ought to do it, and in particular how we might work out a more creative working partnership between the layman and the theologian . . . We all of us feel so very strongly about it . . . I can't remember wanting any person for any job with stronger conviction than I do in this case.

This kind of appeal was difficult to resist. The original notion seems to have been that the members would raise sufficient funds to enable me to live and work in London and make use of the *Christian News-Letter* office and secretariat. I did not warm to this, if only because I have always hated the idea of living and working in London. The offer of the canonry at Windsor put quite a different complexion on the situation. The statutory duties of a canon there are minimal and probably leave more time for outside employments than any other office in the Church. Another consideration that weighed with me was my desire to have a house where my father, who was now nearly eighty and living alone at Rye, could live with me if he wished to do so. In point of fact, though he often stayed with me both at Hawarden and at Windsor, he preferred to go on living at Rye where all his friends and interests were. But it was primarily for the sake of the CFC that I accepted the Windsor canonry. The initial understanding was that I should look after its affairs and spend one day a week in the office in London. Before long, however, the *Christian News-Letter* was closed down, and my house at Windsor became the Frontier Council's office where I had the help of a secretary. I did not want a salary, but the Council paid my travelling and entertaining expenses and the secretary was free to do my personal as well as official correspondence.

In retrospect I think I was somewhat rash in accepting the canonry, although in the event it turned out all right. I had not realized what would be involved in keeping up a large house in Windsor Castle on a stipend of £1000 a year. The house had about twenty rooms and, while it was splendidly situated with a view over the river to Eton, it was not designed for economic management. Moreover, since until now I had needed to furnish no more than a study and bedroom, I was in no ready condition to furnish such a house. However, that difficulty was overcome not only by the purchase of a good deal of second-hand furniture, but by my undertaking to house furniture for some of my friends who could thereby be saved the expense of storage. The chief of these was an American priest, Benjamin Bissell, who had held a living in England and was now returning to work in the USA, but who contemplated coming back to the

Windsor Castle

UK later on, when he would require his furniture again. He was (alas!) murdered in Philadelphia by an importunate beggar on 29 December 1954. His executors readily approved that as I had been storing his furniture I could retain it. There

remained the question what use I was to make of the many
rooms in my house, once I had succeeded in furnishing them.
This problem, as I shall explain, received a solution that I
had by no means foreseen.

St George's Chapel, Windsor, was in my time served by a
dean; three canons;[1] three minor canons, who were responsible
for singing the services but of course had other occupations
as well; the organists, lay clerks and choristers, who constituted
the choir; a staff of vergers and other officials. They all resided
in the castle precincts together with the Military Knights of
Windsor and other people of varying eminence connected with
the Court. All of them taken together (about 200 in number)
were known as the castle community and became more or less
friendly with one another. I particularly enjoyed the society
of the Military Knights and their wives who wholesomely
balanced or counteracted the ecclesiastical preoccupations of
the clergy. But before I arrived at Windsor I prudently
renounced the game of bridge since I perceived that in such a
community I as a single man would constantly be called upon
to make up a four. Social conventions survived at Windsor that
must have been obsolete nearly everywhere else. After I arrived,
a host of visiting cards was left at my house; if your mother-
in-law was ill you turned down a corner of a card, or whatever.
If I had had a wife I should have had to take these conventions
more seriously than I did; as it was, I sat very lightly to them.

The Dean, Eric Hamilton, and his wife were both not only
very good-looking but were as good as they looked. He was a
natural Londoner and had spent most of his life as a parish
priest there. During the war he had been suffragan bishop of
Shrewsbury but had not taken to rural life. He did all that was
required of him as dean gracefully and efficiently, but there was
not enough to employ all his talents and he would have been

1. There should have been four, but one canonry had been suspended for financial reasons. I am glad to say that it has since been
revived.

more happily and usefully employed as bishop of an urban diocese.

When I was appointed, the other two canons were Stafford Crawley and Duncan Armytage. Crawley just had time to send me a kind and welcoming letter before his sudden death on 8 October 1948. Malcolm Venables, who had retired to a country parish in Somerset after being a housemaster at Harrow, was appointed to succeed him, and as the memories of the war were still lively we became known as V1 and V2. Malcolm, as a boy, had been an outstanding chorister at Magdalen College, Oxford, and was well qualified to hold the office of Precentor, that is, to handle the musical side of our corporate responsibilities. I became chapter librarian, which was the least onerous of the canonical offices.

Duncan Armytage was our steward who had oversight of our finances and buildings, and there was a chapter clerk who did the routine work. Duncan was a man of piety and charm with a strong pastoral sense and an active concern with the training of candidates for ordination. But it is a curious fact, perhaps a pure coincidence, that, like his two immediate predecessors in the office of steward, he got across his colleagues. J. N. Dalton (father of Hugh Dalton) had tyrannized over the chapter in his time, and Anthony Deane, who succeeded him in 1931, had made a misery of Eric Hamilton's early days as dean. Duncan Armytage, despite his manifest virtues, was an ecclesiastical fanatic in the manner of Dr Barnes, though his fanaticisms were of a different kind. He was tiresomely obstreperous and unco-operative and liable to sulk if he did not get his way: he thus made himself and other people unhappy.

It is notorious that cathedral and collegiate chapters are prone to be quarrelsome. I once knew a canon of Ely Cathedral (there were six of them then) who was said to be the only one on speaking terms with all the others. I came to understand at Windsor how that state of affairs could arise. Each member of a cathedral or collegiate chapter is likely previously to have been the head of some institution, whether a parish, a diocese, a college or a school, and so finds it very difficult to be in a subordinate position, to act as one of a team, and to bow to collective judgments. I had, as will appear, so many other interests that I was not so much bothered as my colleagues by the inevitable tensions in the cloisters at Windsor Castle, which anyhow ceased to trouble after Duncan Armytage's sudden death in February 1954; he was succeeded by Charles Ritchie, who had been Archdeacon of Northumberland and was the most amiable of colleagues.

As I said, the statutory duties of the dean and canons of Windsor were minimal. None of us could pretend, in Lord Reith's expression, that we were stretched by them. Each canon was 'in residence' for four months in each year, which meant that during those months he was obliged to attend the daily services in the chapel and to preach on Sunday mornings. At other times he was free to be away or to do what he wanted. In practice, we attended the chapel services when we were not in residence unless we had other engagements. Though I have no musical expertise, I cannot say how much I valued the choral services and the singing of the choir under the direction of our distinguished and lovable organist, Dr W. H. Harris. During my early years at Windsor the renowned Dr E. H. Fellowes was still active as a minor canon and I got to know him well. It was a scandal that he had not been made a full canon. It was a pleasure too to have to do with the lay clerks and choristers; some of the latter used to come to tea with me on Sundays. In 1949 Timothy Bavin, at present Bishop of Johannesburg, was the senior chorister.

I must now explain the unforeseen way in which I came to make the fullest possible use of my large house. I had hardly settled in when Duncan Armytage, who was on the Church's council for training men for the ministry, asked me whether I would consider having some middle-aged candidates for holy orders to reside in my house and whether I would direct or supervise their training. I had had some experience of doing this at Hawarden, and it seemed a suitable way of utilizing the accommodation that I found at my disposal. It was understood that the men who would come would be capable of reading on their own and would not require to be spoon-fed, and also that I should be free to work out my own method of training them. I did not propose to charge them anything for teaching or for the supervision of their studies, but what they would pay for their board and lodging would help to make the running of my house economically viable.

I had no sooner expressed my willingness to embark on an experiment of this kind than I began to receive inquiries from bishops about whether I could receive candidates whom they were sponsoring. Within a few months I had six, and later seven, living with me and sharing a common life in my house, and eventually nearly fifty passed through my hands. Towards the end of my time at Windsor I published a detailed account of how this experiment worked out and of the method of training that I devised, including the complete syllabus for a course of five terms (see *Theology*, October 1956, pp. 395–404). I will mention here only a few salient points.

The men who took the course were of about 40 to 60 years of age. They had already had a career in the Army, the Royal Navy, the Merchant Navy, the Civil Service, or as doctors, schoolmasters, income tax inspectors, etc., and wanted to do a useful spell of work in the ordained ministry of the Church before they finally retired. Most of them were married and had to provide for the upkeep of their families while they were with me. I may say that I made it my business to give their wives some good advice when I had the opportunity!

It soon became necessary to find a name, and preferably a monosyllabic one, for these middle-aged ordination candidates. Duncan Armytage wanted them to be known as 'Vidler's vipers'! But I preferred the name 'doves' after 'Vaughan's doves'. That had been the name given to the men who had trained for the ministry in the household of C. J. Vaughan, a well-known Victorian divine, and it so happened that our neighbour, Dr E. H. Fellowes, was one of their last survivors. The name 'doves' at once took on, and I use it here.

I did not lecture to the doves, but I told them what they were to read on the many subjects that we attempted to cover in outline. On two or three evenings each week we held what we called a 'seminar', for which a dove, to whom the task had been assigned, read a short paper on a subject about which they had all been reading, and this was followed by questions and discussion. They also learned a good deal through our general conversation at meals and at other times and through discussion among themselves. Once a week I designated one of them to preach a sermon before the rest of us in a side-chapel in St George's, after which we returned to my house and all had a go at ruthlessly criticizing it. I had been much impressed by this method when I took part in a course at the College of Preachers at Washington DC in 1947. The Dean usually came and assisted in this exercise, which the doves regarded as daunting but which was exceedingly salutary. They were expected to show keen powers of criticizing the preacher's delivery and style as well as the content and structure of his discourse. I was much edified and encouraged by the admirable spirit with which brutally frank and often devastating criticism was made and received, and I was able to perceive term by term consequent progress in the quality of each dove's sermons. All along, I was impressed by the modesty and diffidence with which these widely experienced men pursued their training and by their readiness and eagerness to learn.

As regards prayer and worship, we had the great advantage of making use of St George's Chapel. I naturally impressed upon the doves the importance of a disciplined way and rule of life, which would not, as in many other professions, be imposed upon them. From time to time I got friends of mine to come and speak to them about special topics such as marriage guidance, the teaching of the young, ministry in country parishes, etc. They also gained some practical experience by taking services and preaching on Sundays in parishes around Windsor. When the time came for their ordination they either wrote essays for their bishops or took a deacon's examination and, so far as I remember, they all came through with flying colours or at any rate without discredit.

For the most part they first served as curates for two or three years in a town parish and then were appointed to a country parish of their own. I kept in touch with them, and do to this day with those who are still alive, and we had periodical reunions. I was greatly heartened when I visited them to find what good work they were doing and how much their parishioners appreciated them (some of them became rural deans!). I consider that training doves has been the most worth-while thing that I have done in my life, and I hope that it may compensate for some of my own deficiencies as a clerk in holy orders.

The coming of the doves made it necessary for me to establish efficient and smooth domestic arrangements in my house. This was not easily done. I had an awkward start. My predecessor's family, who were to have vacated the house in October, did not actually vacate it till the very day on which I arrived at Windsor (16 December 1948). Only two rooms had been prepared for me; all the others had to be redecorated and repaired after I was installed. Then the good woman whom I had engaged to become my cook-housekeeper let me down at the last moment, and I had to take on a man, Albert Dews by name, who had also answered my advertisement and who said that he had previously kept house for unmarried priests. His great ambition was to run a café (pronounced 'caff'). His heart was stronger than his head and his accomplishments as a cook were as minimal as the statutory duties of a canon of Windsor. He was also subject to violent explosions of temper, but I quite liked him and kept up with him till his death many years later.

He affected to be a keen High Churchman, but did not seem to do much about it. He was put out when, to help him, I engaged another man of melancholy disposition who was very religious in practice as well as in theory and spent most of his time reading *The Church Times* in the kitchen. He did not last for long, nor indeed could poor Albert. At this juncture Mrs Mary Pearce, whom I had known when she had taken a course at William Temple College, Hawarden, and who, like her daughter Joyce Pearce the founder of the Ockenden Venture, was a fount of beneficence, came to preside over my domestic arrangements for a time. But unfortunately she could not get servants to stay with her. I was told that they like to work for a single man rather than for a woman who is more likely to boss them about and tell them where they get off.

My problem was finally solved when the invaluable Mrs Smithers appeared on the scene. For the rest of my time at Windsor, with the help of a housemaid, she managed everything with tireless competence and unflagging devotion. She became much attached to the doves whom she regarded as her 'boys' and was never known to complain of the very substantial demands made upon her – although we did make our own beds and waited upon ourselves at meals, and had a rota of duties for the purpose.

I may have given the impression that training doves replaced or interfered with the work that I had undertaken to do for the Christian Frontier Council, but this was not at all the case. I usually went up to London on about two days a week for the middle of the day or for the evening, according to the time when I had meetings to attend or other engagements. The Frontier Council itself met for dinner and a meeting about once a month. It was my business to invite the proposed speaker and some other experts on the subject to be considered and to make any other needful arrangements. We had at least one weekend conference each year away from London, which the members much valued. In addition, I served a number of specialist groups that met at other times, for example, doctors, educationalists, and industrialists. We also took to holding frontier luncheons in London, at which members of the council were able to communicate their ideas to a larger public: these proved to be a considerable success. Then I also became with Philip Mairet co-editor of a monthly magazine, called *The Frontier*, which took the place of the *Christian News-Letter*, as our organ. He did the bulk of the editorial work, but it naturally took up some of my time too.

There were other extra-mural activities in which I engaged while I was at Windsor as I had done at Hawarden. I continued to edit *Theology*, but I need say no more about that. I was also from time to time still invited to conduct university missions but except for the one at Durham in 1951 I found that I could not be absent in term time from Windsor for the required periods. I was however able to accept an invitation from the Divinity Faculty at Cambridge to give a course of open theological lectures, such as Dr J. S. Whale had earlier done (see his book, *Christian Doctrine*), on Saturday mornings in the Michaelmas term 1949. They were largely attended and were afterwards published with the title *Christian Belief* (1950), a book that went through several editions.

A more attractive invitation was that from the Council of Trinity College, Cambridge, to give the Birkbeck Lectures in ecclesiastical history in 1953. I say 'more attractive' because I have always been happier in writing history than in theologizing. In this case I had for years wanted to write a book about that fascinating and prophetic figure in France's ecclesiastical history, Félicité de La Mennais or Lamennais. This invitation provided me with an occasion to bring my desire to fruition, and I derived much pleasure from researching into the voluminous literature of the subject, in visiting the scenes of Lamennais's activity, and in using the Mennaisian archives at Highlands on the island of Jersey, where I stayed during two of the doves' vacations. My book, *Prophecy and Papacy: a study of Lamen-*

nais, the Church and the Revolution (1954) was kindly received by historians and at one time I contemplated writing a sequel on Lamennais's career after his rupture with the Church. But I was diverted to other tasks.

I was also invited to give the Firth Memorial Lectures at Nottingham University in 1955, to which I gave the title *Christian Belief and this World* (1956); this book is partly a sequel to *Christian Belief*, but mainly an attempt to articulate a theology for the Christian Frontier. I had previously used some of the material for the Sir D. Owen Evans lectures at University College, Aberystwyth.

In September 1955 I was asked to lead a delegation of Anglican theologians who were to have a series of meetings with a corresponding number of Roman Catholic theologians in order to explore questions of doctrine together, without intending to formulate any concrete proposals for unity. The Anglicans had previously been led by Dr G. L. Prestige, who had died. I felt I ought to do this. We had periodical residential meetings, sometimes in England, sometimes in Italy. Although both the Pope and the Archbishop of Canterbury took cognisance and approved of what we were doing, neither gave any public recognition to our activities which were indeed to be conducted in the utmost secrecy.

Nowadays such conversations are commonplace and are publicized, but in those days, before the Second Vatican Council, it was supposed that publicity about them might give rise to the same sort of controversy as had been caused by the Malines Conversations in the 1920s. I have a large file of documentation about our conversations which those of us who took part in them found both instructive and rewarding. They were held in a very friendly atmosphere, and it was interesting to observe that differences of theological opinion often cut across ecclesiastical allegiances. When I had to give up my part in these proceedings, I was rather surprised to receive no word of appreciation or gratitude from Lambeth

Palace, for we had devoted a lot of time and thought to them and also had incurred some expense.

Naturally, while I was at Windsor I took part in many august ceremonies. Each year in June there was the annual service of the Order of the Garter, a magnificent piece of pageantry, to which over the years I was able to invite a large number of my friends. Then I took part in the funerals of King George VI and of Queen Mary, and was present at the coronation of Queen Elizabeth II. I will say nothing about the kindly way in which I was entertained by the royal family when the court was in residence in the castle, lest I succumb to the temptations of a Crawfie!

My life at Windsor also had its lighter side. I was induced by the doves to take up the game of golf of which I soon became an addict. As I had access to the private golf course in the home park, I was able to take golf-playing doves there for a round on most afternoons. Very few other people played on the course in those days, so that we usually had it to ourselves, which spoilt me for the future use of crowded public links. On Saturdays the doves had a day off and I insisted on their going out or away for the day, so that I was able to entertain other friends in my house; members of the Frontier Council and others would come to see me then. On Saturday evenings I went pretty regularly to the Theatre Royal, Windsor, which was within a stone's throw of my house and maintained a very high standard. I usually had a house party at Christmas. Members of my family, the Muggeridges, and African students, were among the guests who joined me then. There was no dearth of social life in Windsor and I made many new friends.

After Duncan Armytage's death I became Steward and found that office full of interest. I had many conferences with Lord Mottistone who was our architect not only about the fabric and furnishings of St George's Chapel but about the numerous other buildings for which we were responsible. I looked forward, as I had done at Hawarden, to spending the rest of my working days at Windsor, and as there was no retiring age for canons there is no telling how long I might have continued to enjoy the extremely agreeable conditions of my life there. But I suppose that from 1954, when my father died at the age of eighty-four, I took it for granted that in the end I should return to Rye to live in the house in which I had been born and which he bequeathed to me.

CHAPTER X

Dean of King's

It was on 31 May 1956 that, out of the blue, I received a letter from the Vice-Provost of King's College, Cambridge, asking whether I was willing to be considered for the post of dean. It was the Vice-Provost who wrote because the college had recently been bereaved of its provost (Stephen Glanville) as well as of its dean (Ivor Ramsay). I had never met either of them, and had had no previous connection with King's, except that I had often worshipped in the college chapel and had been closely associated with Eric Milner-White who had been dean from 1918 to 1941.

Ivor Ramsay had fallen from the roof of the chapel on a stormy night in January. The circumstances were mysterious and it was not clear whether his death had been accidental or deliberate. So far as I could gather, he had had an unworldly, Franciscan type of character, and was generally revered on account of his piety and kindliness, though he may have been mocked by some of his colleagues for intellectual naivety. He was a Scot and had been provost of St Mary's Cathedral, Edinburgh. I was told that his first sermon as Dean of King's had had a strongly Jacobite flavour.

Stephen Glanville, who had been Professor of Egyptology in the university, was evidently a man greatly beloved in King's. He had become provost only in 1954 and his early death had been a severe blow. These distressing losses that King's had lately sustained lent a forceful edge, which otherwise it might have lacked, to the invitation that I had so unexpectedly received.

It was not an easy decision to make. There was little to choose between the attractions of St George's Chapel and King's College Chapel. Both were superbly beautiful buildings, King's Chapel the more magnificent, St George's with a much richer range of historical interest. Both were served by deservedly famous choirs. I had no wish to move from Windsor and considered that I was doing as useful a work in training doves there as I was ever likely to do anywhere. Then, the amenities of life in Windsor Castle, which included access to the home park for walking and a private golf course, were not likely to be surpassed, or even equalled, elsewhere, and there was the prospect that I might be able to continue to enjoy them into a ripe old age!

On the other hand, it was obviously an invitation that I had to take very seriously. By the time I went to Cambridge to talk the matter over, the new provost (Noël Annan) had been elected. I took to him at once and was more than satisfied with what I learned about the conditions under which I should be living and working, though naturally the provision of a private golf course could not be numbered among them. I was quite sure that, if I had to make a move, I should prefer an academic to an ecclesiastical appointment. I may remark here that I was astonished by the number of people who wrote to me at this time to say that they had got me earmarked for the deanery of St Paul's or words to that effect. Indeed my journal reminds me that in March 1955 a Jesuit friend had told me that he *prayed* (!) that I would be the next dean of St Paul's: to that I had appended the words *mē genoito* (usually translated 'God forbid'). I suppose that I ought to have felt flattered in view of the eminent men from John Donne to R. W. Church, W. R. Inge and W. R. Matthews, who had occupied the position, but my dislike of London was so intense that the very suggestion appalled me.

It is true that, so far as its fellows were concerned, King's had in some quarters the reputation of being a den or nest of atheists, but I had known Milner-White too well to believe or to be daunted by that. In point of fact, as regards religious beliefs and unbeliefs, King's high table, like other academic societies, reflected the attitudes of the time that were fashionable or coming to be fashionable and was anything but monochrome. After I had been at King's for a term, I confided to one of the younger fellows that I had encountered none of the hostility or suspicion that some people had warned me to expect; he, being of a facetious turn of mind, replied: 'Oh, but you wait till X returns who is away on sabbatical leave this year; then you'll be for it!' X did return and became one of my closest friends and collaborators.

It was of course anomalous that a Christian institution like King's Chapel should be the responsibility of, and controlled by, the governing body (that is, eighty or more fellows) of a necessarily creedless or pluralistic college. But this is one of those happy anomalies with which the English have long been familiar and which they know how to work satisfactorily. One aspect of this anomaly was that King's, like other colleges and like the university itself, was patron of a considerable number of benefices in the Church of England and nominated new incumbents when vacancies occurred. I had had a good deal of experience of purely ecclesiastical patronage and I can testify that the college's Church patronage committee showed itself to be an excellent judge of parsons. Despite whatever ecclesiastical purists may say, the Church should account itself fortunate to be able to retain this form of patronage as long as possible. Incidentally, the college was able to help its parishes financially from generous funds that in the past had been bequeathed for the purpose. During vacations I used to visit our college livings and keep in touch with the incumbents, who also received the annual gift of a theological book from the college.

In reality the main characteristic of King's was not atheism or any other 'ism, but a genuine liberality. I noted that at the first dinner for old Kingsmen that I attended (28 September 1957) the provost said that the chief things for which King's stood were friendship and esteem for knowledge and wisdom. I applauded, and the better I got to know the college the more I agreed. As regards friendship, the relations between dons and undergraduates were much more free and easy than I had observed in other colleges. For example, the fellows did not hive off into a separate room for lunch but sat among the undergraduates. Altogether I quickly found the atmosphere or ethos, or whatever you call it, entirely to my taste. The high regard in which intellectual integrity and acumen, and honesty, and tolerance, were held was as welcome as it was stimulating. One of the main reasons why I accepted the invitation to go to King's was that I should be more extended or stretched there than I was in the agreeable and easy-going environment of Windsor.

My appointment took effect from Michaelmas 1956, but the college allowed me to remain at Windsor for that term so that I could round off the training of the doves to whom I was committed. Thus during the Michaelmas term I went to Cambridge only for special occasions like the annual meeting of the governing body and the Advent carol service. I finally moved on 18 December into entrancing rooms in Bodley's Court down by the river, from which there was a view on one side of the Cam and of Clare bridge and on the other of the old buildings of Queens' College. Of course I could use only a small amount of the furniture that I had assembled at Windsor, but I was able to lend some of the remainder to friends who would house it and use it till I needed it again.

I have been writing as though there was only one dean of King's, but the college statutes required that there should be two. By convention one of them was in holy orders and had special responsibilities with regard to the chapel and its services; the other was usually a young unmarried fellow who was resident in college and who had special responsibilities with regard to King's College School where the choristers and a lot of other boys as well were educated. The succession of lay deans in my time, with whom my relations could not have been happier, was John Barton (afterwards the Shakespearean producer at Stratford), James Cargill-Thompson (now Professor of Ecclesiastical History at King's College, London), and Philip Brett (now a professor of music in the USA).

Since the deans were jointly responsible for the maintenance of discipline in the college, one of us had always to be in residence. We were each on duty for half of each term, and during our periods of duty had to be available every day to undergraduates to sign exeats and late leaves which in those days were required by any who wanted to be away for a night or out of college after midnight. They may have found this requirement irksome, but from my point of view it had the advantage that sooner or later all undergraduates came to my rooms and I could more easily get to know them. I signed whatever they wanted with a quill pen which Americans thought very cute and even asked to photograph.

As regards discipline, I do not know how it may be now, but we reckoned then that if undergraduates were treated as mature adults they were the more likely to behave as such. I remember, soon after I went to King's, going round the bounds of the college with my fellow dean and the tutor and directing that such brutal impediments to climbing in as superfluous spikes and broken glass should be removed. There had to be some impediments so that we could assure the university that our undergraduates had spent the requisite number of nights in residence each term.

Before I say anything more about my duties and tasks at King's I will mention two personal matters. Ever since I had been made a DD of Edinburgh university in 1946 I had come to be known as 'Dr Vidler', but the degrees of Scottish and other universities were not recognized at Cambridge, so that, if I was not to sail under false colours, I had to apply for a Cambridge

OVERLEAF *The Library of the Friars of the Sack*

doctorate. I therefore submitted some of my historical writings for the degree of Litt.D. I may add that I had always had an aversion for 'canon' as a title. I took the old-fashioned view that it was an office, not a title. When I was made an honorary canon of Derby Cathedral in 1946 I got the Bishop (A. E. J. Rawlinson) to promise that I should not be made a canon emeritus when I vacated the office, and fortunately at Windsor there was no machinery at all for making a canon emeritus. Although since 1956 some ill-informed people have addressed me as 'canon', they have had no warrant whatever for doing so and I have regarded them with distaste.

The other personal matter was not purely personal, is of more interest, and needs more explanation. I had always understood from Milner-White that King's Chapel and the clergy who served it were exempt from normal ecclesiastical jurisdiction because of a bull that had been issued by a pope at the time of the foundation of the college. We had of course an official 'Visitor', who was *ex officio* the Bishop of Lincoln, and that was as much episcopal supervision as we needed. He visited King's once a year to take a confirmation service, but otherwise we gave him little to do. I was aware that for some time the bishops of Ely, in whose diocese Cambridge is situated, had been trying to extend their control over the deans and chaplains of the colleges by getting them to apply for a licence to officiate. I had no intention of abandoning or compromising the traditional independence of King's, but in order to acquire some formal status in the Church of England as a whole, it occurred to me that I might ask the university to bring into operation an old procedure by which it was entitled to license a number of its members in holy orders to preach throughout England without their needing permission from diocesan bishops. This right derived from a statute of the reign of Queen Elizabeth I, and although no clergyman had received, or perhaps applied for, the licence for over a century, I was eager that the right should not disappear through disuse.

I therefore submitted an application for the university's licence to preach throughout England. My application had to go before the council of the senate whose members, I was given to understand, found it a curious and interesting variation of their normal business, all the more interesting since it was learned that the Archbishop of Canterbury (Fisher) was averse to my application's being granted. The next step I will record in an extract from my journal for 23 February 1957:

I called on the Vice-Chancellor (B. W. Downs, Master of Christ's College) at his request about my application for the university's licence to preach. He asked whether I realized it was a university, not a Vice-Chancellor's, licence; therefore it would be a public matter requiring a grace of the senate, etc. I said I was quite prepared for that and indeed welcomed it. He also said that they hadn't yet discovered what the form of the licence should be exactly but inquiries were proceeding. One was last issued in the 18th century for the founder of the SPG, I think he said, whose name neither of us could recall at the moment. Then he asked whether I would tell him informally what were my reasons for applying, which I said I would gladly do. I said these were (i) I get many invitations to preach all over England and it would be a convenience to me and those who invite me if I were covered in this way, (ii) I have twice been refused permission to preach by diocesan bishops, one because I was regarded as too High Church, and the other because I was regarded as too Low Church, (iii) I regard it as important in the interests of liberty within the Church that this right of the university should exist not only on paper but be in running order, and I am better placed for getting such a licence than some quite young man, (iv) I also want to ascertain whether the university meant business when it recently got this right recognized in the proposed revised canons when the ecclesiastical authorities were trying to remove it: I am apprehensive of the attempt of the hierarchy to get regimenting powers in their own hands. I didn't add that a final motive is that the Archbishop of Canterbury will be annoyed!

After further deliberation the council of the senate agreed to promote a 'grace', that is, a formal vote of the university, that the licence for which I had applied should be granted. But that was not the end of the matter. The vote in the senate house was to be taken after lunch on Saturday 1 June. I could not be present myself as I was out to lunch, but a rumour had reached me beforehand that the vote might be opposed and I was advised to arrange that some of my friends should be present to see it through. In consequence the Provost and about a dozen fellows of King's, including E. M. Forster, had gone along to make sure that their dean was licensed to preach throughout England! The Provost told me afterwards that he had felt like a Tammany boss arriving a bit late to see that all his guys were there! In the event the opposition had not materialized.

The final curiosity in this affair was when I went to the registrary's office to sign the ancient book in which those who had received the university's licence signified their assent to the thirty-nine articles of religion. The form of assent for me to sign had been copied out from the last entry which spoke of 'the United Church of England and Ireland'. I pointed out that since 1869 the Church of Ireland had been disestablished and separated from the Church of England. The registrary said: 'Oh! but can't we use the old form?' I said that I should be overjoyed, since I should never get another chance of signing anything like that!

To return to my duties as dean. When I had first conferred with the Provost and some of the fellows, I had said with the chapel and its services in mind that, while I was by disposition a reformer and inclined to promote well-considered experiments and innovations, I should not come with any doctrinaire ideas and should not urge any changes until I had had plenty of time to take full stock of the existing state of affairs. In particular, I realized that King's Chapel had two distinguishable functions: on the one hand, it should serve as effectively as possible as the chapel of the present members of the college, but on the other hand it was a great national institution to which people came from far and wide and, like other collegiate churches and cathedrals, it was responsible for maintaining at the highest possible level the musical and liturgical traditions of the Church of England. Thus, while in many parish churches and in other college chapels I might want to initiate a good deal of change, at King's I was likely to be much more conservative.

In any case, since I laid no claim to musical expertise, I would not seek to interfere with the responsibilities of the organists and directors of music. When I came to King's, it is sad to relate that Boris Ord's health was already gravely impaired, so that it was with David Willcocks that I had the pleasure of co-operating almost from the beginning. Musicians as a class are said to be temperamental and to be liable to go off the deep end about one thing or another. If this is so, David Willcocks was exceptional, for no one could have been more uniformly or consistently easy to work with. I do not recall that we ever had a cross word. I was equally fortunate in each of the college chaplains of my time, namely David Isitt, Peter Cameron and William Leah, who were responsible not only for singing the choral services, as the minor canons had been at Windsor, but also for pastoral work among the under-graduates.

Any alterations or innovations we wanted to make in the chapel needed to be approved by the college council. I got it to agree to my forming a chapel consultative committee that was broadly representative of senior and junior members of the college, which met regularly to make and consider suggestions and whose recommendations I could bring to the council. I received every kind of encouragement and never met with any obstruction. One of the innovations we started was the reading of 'homilies' by fellows of the college at choral matins on Sundays, that is, select passages from great religious literature. We also started having sung eucharists instead of evensong on such days as Ascension day and All Souls day. This was before evening masses had become customary. We experimented with various forms of service for undergraduates, some of which hit the mark better than others.

My predecessors from Milner-White onwards had, I believe, always had one evening a week in term time when they were 'at home' in their rooms to those undergraduates who were communicants or committed Christians or under instruction and who on these occasions received further enlightenment and confirmation in the faith. I know that many of them were permanently grateful for the benefits they derived from these gatherings. They also became a closely-knit group in the college through their attendance at the 'saints' breakfast after the early communion on Sundays. On the other hand, the impression was created that the Dean had a special, if not an exclusive, concern for this group within the college, which was given such nicknames as 'the God-boys'.

I decided to disturb or to break through this impression, notably by arranging with my fellow dean that we would have a joint 'at home' on one evening a week and would invite fellows of the college and others to come and open a discussion on some subject that they could speak about with special authority. These 'at homes' were held in my rooms which were better suited for the purpose and could accommodate about fifty at a push. They proved to be popular. Attendances naturally varied, but often we were crowded to capacity, for instance, on the first Thursday in each Michaelmas term when Sir John Sheppard (the former Provost who was still in residence) regularly spoke about his 'Reminiscences of King's', or when E. M. Forster came to speak as he often did, or when someone like Dean Acheson was staying in college and spent an evening with us. I also arranged that on another occasion in each week we had a discussion group for senior and junior members of the college which concentrated on religious and ethical questions.

Apart from that, I became director of studies in theology and usually had about half a dozen pupils reading for parts of the theological tripos as well as research students to supervise. Their level of performance varied of course: 1965 was notable because of my four pupils who took the tripos that year two got firsts and the other two II.1s. I also did a good deal of supervision in modern Church history of undergraduates from other colleges. On two mornings a week I took a divinity class at King's College School and each year I had a number of boys to prepare for confirmation. On Sunday afternoons after evensong four choristers used to come to tea in my rooms and afterwards we would play Scrabble, a game to which Dr John Robinson had introduced me. I enjoyed this contact with the school as I had done with St George's School at Windsor.

In 1958 when Owen Chadwick succeeded Norman Sykes as Dixie Professor of Ecclesiastical History, there was a vacancy for a university lecturer in modern Church history and I was invited to fill it. I judged that I was already so fully occupied that I could take on this additional work only if my duties in King's were substantially reduced, especially during the initial years when I should have many fresh lectures to prepare. The college kindly agreed to appoint a second chaplain (to be known as 'the succentor', though this did not imply musical accomplishments!) who took over many of my college tasks in connection with the chapel and school. My friend, Victor de Waal, now Dean of Canterbury, held this office from 1959 to 1963, by which time I found that I could manage again without such assistance.

As a university lecturer I also became a member of the faculty board of divinity, and for two years served as chairman of that body. Before accepting the chairmanship, I asked that the practice of starting meetings with prayer should be dropped. It was a former Ely Professor of Divinity and Provost of King's (A. E. Brooke) who had observed that the faculty board of divinity was the only one that opened its meetings with prayer and whose members then immediately started to quarrel! My proposal for dropping prayers, which was accepted, had nothing to do with quarrels which by this time had for the most part ceased, but was motivated by the consideration that there were no religious tests for members of the faculty and it ought not to be assumed in a pluralistic or non-confessional university that everyone could conscientiously join in prayer.

I also served on a number of university syndicates, of which much the most interesting was the press syndicate, which decided on all the books that were to be published by the Cambridge University Press. The press syndicate met on the same afternoon in the week as King's College council, so that I became dispensed from membership of the latter for some years. Nevertheless, I always took an active interest in college business, and on one occasion at least had a (to me) memorable triumph in a matter that was off my normal beat.

The area in front of the porter's lodge on King's Parade needed reconstruction as the cobbles were in a very bad way. The college council consulted an eminent architect who recommended that the area should be reconstructed with granite sets instead of with cobbles. When the council brought this recommendation to the governing body I opposed it vigorously and said that it would make the entrance to the college look like the entrance to a municipal swimming bath. Consequently the proposal was referred back to the council for reconsideration. But the council in due course returned with a reiteration of its previous recommendation, alleging that the eminent architect had said that cobbles were no longer manufactured! With my home background in Rye, I knew more about cobbles and how they came into existence than the eminent architect did, and when the matter next came before the governing body I made the speech of my life. The result was that the council's recommendation was overwhelmingly rejected and an admirable scheme for recobbling, designed by Michael Jaffé, was adopted.

From the time when Rubens' great picture, 'The Adoration of the Magi', was offered to the college in 1961 I was much involved in the protracted discussions about whether and how it could be satisfactorily placed in the chapel. All I need say about this is that I was in favour of the decisions that were finally taken by the governing body and carried into effect after my retirement.

While I was at King's I continued to do some historical writing which arose in part out of invitations to give courses of lectures in other universities – the Scott Holland and Maurice lectures at King's College, London, the Robertson lectures in Glasgow University, and the Sarum lectures at Oxford. *A Century of Social Catholicism* (1964) and *20th Century Defenders of the Faith* (1965) originated in this way, as well as an enlarged version of my book on Maurice, *F. D. Maurice and Company* (1966), and later *A Variety of Catholic Modernists* (1970) was to do so too. The last was a sequel to my earlier work, *The Modernist Movement in the Roman Church* (see p. 82).

Soon after my return to Cambridge I had published, with the title *Essays in Liberality* (1957), a collection of my lectures and essays, some of which had previously appeared in periodicals, and also a selection from the sermons that I had preached in St George's Chapel, namely *Windsor Sermons* (1958), of which I still hear echoes. But the most successful of the books that I wrote at this period, to judge by its continuing sales, was *The Church in an Age of Revolution* (1961), which was volume five in 'The Pelican History of the Church'. I believe that it has been widely used as a text-book in colleges and schools.

I spent part of two long vacations in the USA and Canada, mainly on holiday, though I did some lecturing in Chicago,

Toronto and Saskatoon. I had some time in the Medical Centre
at Chicago where my friend Richard Young was episcopalian
chaplain, and while I was there had the opportunity of witnessing open-heart surgery. He was good enough to drive me right
across the States to San Francisco and the West Coast, and on
our return via North Dakota we visited a wealthy friend of his
who owned a large estate in Minnesota. She had three private
aeroplanes and other luxuries to which I was not accustomed.
One day she found that she was without any English mustard
and asked us to fly up into Canada to get some at Kenora,
Ontario. I was invited to return to Minnesota the next year to
do some writing in quietude, to bathe, and to go fishing for
bass in the lakes with a splendid old Pole who managed the
estate, all of which I found to be extremely pleasurable.

Early in 1963 I bought two derelict labourer's cottages in
the country near Shepreth about eight miles south of Cambridge,
and had them made into a modest residence where I could spend
the vacations and have people to stay with me. With my partial-
ity for the letter 'Z', I named it Zoar Cottage. I did a lot of
work in the garden and transferred there my bees which I had
previously kept in a friend's garden at Grantchester. I had been
a beekeeper since 1940 at Hawarden. At Windsor my predecessor's wife, Mrs Ollard, had been one too and I was able
to take over a platform which had been constructed for her
hives on the cliff beneath the canons' houses.

I had from about the age of thirty looked forward to the time
when I should be able to retire. I suppose that I was deficient
in the will to power or to managing other people. Anyhow I
was safeguarded from any temptation to hang on to responsibility too long, since university lecturers at Cambridge were
obliged to retire at the age of sixty-seven. On 14 June 1964 this
entry occurs in my journal:

had a talk with the provost about plans for retiring. I said
I should like some relaxation of work before Sep. 1967

when I should retire altogether; and that I should like to retire from my college offices in Sep. 1966, but would continue my university lectureship till Sep. 1967 if it was thought it would be useful to my successor to have me available during his first year, though I should keep out of the way and not seek to interfere at all and probably reside in my cottage at Shepreth. I said I thought the college would be needing a younger and fresher dean.

This indicates what in fact I was able to do. In the summer of 1966 I took a sabbatical term's leave and, among other diversions, went on an Hellenic cruise with my old friend, Mrs Prior, universally known as 'Pop'. We visited some of the scenes that I was later to cover in company with Malcolm Muggeridge. During the eighteen months before I retired in August 1967 I lived out at Shepreth, going into Cambridge just for lecturing, supervising and the occasional meeting. This enabled me to enjoy the rustic existence for which I had had a nostalgia ever since my boyhood days at Clover cottage, Icklesham. Some of my pupils came to stay with me in order to work during vacations and other friends were able to visit me, including my sister who was now a widow and helped me to settle in at Zoar Cottage. I was sorry to give the cottage up when I retired, but I could find no justification for retaining it.

CAMBRIDGE, FAREWELL!

*A sermon preached in Great St Mary's, Cambridge
on 28 May 1967*

On 1 December 1861 Bertrand Russell's father, Lord Amberley, who was then an undergraduate at Trinity College, wrote a letter to one of his sisters. Among other things he told her that he was going to a party given by the Vice-Chancellor 'who with an extraordinary degree of malice sent his invitations so early that it was impossible to refuse.' About that kind of malice the present Vicar of Great St Mary's has nothing to learn from the then Vice-Chancellor! Even so, he must have tackled me at a moment when I was off my guard, for I do not at all approve of farewell sermons, and hitherto, when leaving one place for another, I have always declined to preach one. In my view, preachers should disappear silently and unobtrusively. I would have them be like Philip the Evangelist – caught away suddenly so that you don't know where they are, until they are found at Azotus or some such place (Acts 8: 39f.).

Only once did I come near to preaching a farewell sermon, and that, I must admit, turned out to be the most effective, perhaps the only effective, sermon I have ever preached. It was when I was leaving Hawarden in North Wales where for nearly ten years I had been Warden of St Deiniol's Library – the most agreeable job in the world. The rector of the parish asked me to preach before I left, and I said I would, provided it was not a 'farewell sermon'. In the course of my allocution, the main theme of which I cannot recall, I took occasion to say what I thought of the pulpit in Hawarden church. It was the pulpit beneath which the great Mr Gladstone had sat with his deaf ears cupped to catch the least words that fell from the lips of the newest curate. It was a massive stone pulpit with the elaborate ornamentation dear to Victorian church restorers. It was not only hideous but, adding injury to insult, it was so constructed that considerable acrobatic skill (such as I do not myself possess) was required in order to get into it. Well, I told the people of Hawarden what I thought about their toleration of this deplorable object, though I did not suppose that my remarks would have any more effect than they usually do. To my astonishment, when I revisited Hawarden two or three years later, I found that the old pulpit had been demolished and replaced by a handsome wooden one which moreover was easy of access, and I was told that this change had been set in motion by my parting words.

This is a record which I cannot expect to repeat. In any case I would die in the last ditch for the preservation of this curious pulpit on wheels in which I am now standing. I may, however, remark in passing that I can conceive myself wishing that, in this as in many other churches, I might return one day and find beneath some of the stained-glass windows inscriptions as follows: 'To the glory of God and in memory of . . . a stained-glass window was removed here in the year . . .'

Farewell sermons, when they are not sentimental, tend, I fancy, to be reminiscent, reflective, or hortatory. I am not against reminiscence. I have so much enjoyed getting my elders to tell me about people and events which they remembered but I was too young to have known, that I easily persuade myself that my juniors like to hear about things and people which I remember but they cannot have known. It happens that I have spent more of my life in Cambridge than anywhere else, though I am thankful that I have also spent much of it in very different environments. I could thus, for example, tell you about some of the once famous but now more or less forgotten men whom I have heard preaching from this pulpit.

Charles Gore preached here for a whole week when I was an undergraduate. He had many of the qualities of a prophet. Lest we should be over-impressed by him, I remember Professor Bethune-Baker (whom everyone knew as the Bath Bun) saying in a lecture that when Bishop Gore rose on his feet and declared (as he frequently did), 'I am profoundly convinced that . . .', we were not to suppose that it was equivalent to an Old Testament prophet's proclaiming, 'Thus saith the Lord'. Again, I can remember W. R. Inge, Dean of St Paul's, who despite his dreary delivery always drew a very large congregation, telling us how in disgust he had thrown Aldous Huxley's *Brave New World* into the Adriatic. I can even remember as a freshman hearing Handley Moule, Bishop of Durham, preaching here shortly before his death. He was a very holy man but not, I believe, a good bishop, which perhaps goes without saying. The preacher who beyond all others impressed me in my undergraduate days was Frank Weston, Bishop of Zanzibar, a great man if ever there was one. Read his life by Maynard Smith some time, if you have not done so. Of course, I also remember other than ecclesiastical figures who are now more or less legendary, such as Sir J. J. Thomson, Master of Trinity. I vividly recall seeing him gazing abstractedly into a shop window which contained nothing but ladies' underwear. I do not think reminiscence is a line I should pursue any further.

What about being reflective? I might reflect upon the changes that have taken place in Cambridge during the half-century in which I have known it. But I am not much inclined to do that. While there have certainly been changes and developments in many directions, I am much more struck by the extent to which, in what is said to be an era of unprecedented change, the university and colleges have so far gone on in much the same way. This is not to deny that altogether more far-reaching changes may be impending in the proximate future. As regards the persons who comprise the university, I should say that the dons are probably more virtuous but less colourful than they used to be, and that while the undergraduates (to speak with moderation) do not look nearly as nice as they did yet behind the appearances I find them for the most part more congenial.

As regards religion, I have witnessed various fashions and fluctuations. But I am sceptical about all generalizations concerning religious conditions in Cambridge or indeed in the country as a whole. I do not at all mind those who are averse to religion supposing and saying that the churches are being rapidly evacuated though, so far as I can make out, this is far from being the case. Nor do I think it likely to be the case unless some much more formidable rival faith emerges than is observable at present. Should that happen, I should not be surprised if it then appeared that there is much more latent, if unconventional, Christian faith in our society, and not least in our university, than meets the eye. In any case the truth of a faith is much more important than its popularity.

Here too greater changes may be impending than any I have witnessed. But for the present I do not find myself being carried away, or being particularly excited, by the contemporary apologists for, or critics of, the Christian faith. And, as for the Church, I am by nature of a gloomy disposition, twenty or thirty years ago I was talking about *ecclesia moribunda*, whereas now I find that I am much less melancholy than those churchmen to whom, I suppose, it is a new idea. For myself I welcome the prospect of retirement and quietude. Possibly some more worthwhile reflections will occur to me then.

Am I then to become hortatory and to offer you the fruits of experience in the form of good advice? That would be most distasteful of all. I cannot endure preachers when they are obviously trying to get at you, or doing propaganda for this or that, or drawing morals and telling you plainly what you ought to do. If we must have preachers, I like them to be oblique and reserved and even enigmatic.

Here, for instance, is a story which in my opinion constitutes an oblique comment on academic existence in this home of culture. It is a story that was told by one religious philosopher to another.

In the 1890s Baron Friedrich von Hügel, who was a Roman Catholic layman, called on, and had his one and only talk with, Dr James Martineau, the greatest unitarian divine of the century. Martineau was then over 90 years of age, but still very much alive. At the end of their conversation he told von Hügel this story, and I'll tell it in what I take to have been Martineau's own words.

'In that chair in which you are sitting,' he said, 'there sat a few weeks ago a man in whose case I think you will be interested. A little over a year ago he first came to see me –

without any introduction. He was an American in his thirties, in vigorous health and highly educated. He said that he had long known me by repute and from my writings as an honest man – as a believer, it is true, but as a believer in not over-much. He had come to Europe, and to see me, because he was perplexed and wanted sound advice. He said that, after taking his degree, since he had ample wealth, he had found himself free to do with his life whatever he thought most serviceable.

'At that time, he had not only been without any religious belief, but had been completely convinced that religion was an illusion and extremely harmful. He had therefore decided to devote himself to its eradication. For ten years now he had been going around speaking and lecturing – with much apparent success. Nothing in particular had happened, so far as he could tell, to make him hesitate to go on with this good work. Yet in recent months he had been disturbed in his mind by questions such as these: "How can you be so sure that all the various religions, even in what they jointly affirm, are purely, foolishly and demonstrably deluded? Isn't it just possible that you are mistaken? Why not suspend your pro-paganda for a time and re-study the whole question? Why not get away to Europe and procure an opinion about what to do and how to act?" And so he concluded, "What would you do, Dr Martineau, in such a case as mine?"

'After due reflection, this is the advice that Dr Martineau gave him. "If I were in your position," he said, "since I could afford to do so, I should take a year to carry out a double experiment. I would spend the whole year among people of the same race. The first six months I should spend among the most traditionally minded persons of this race – traditional not least in their religious faith and practice – persons without the charm of intellectual culture, without quick wittedness or breadth of sympathy or modern elasticity. The second six months I should spend among persons of the same race but the most emancipated from all religious traditions and convictions, and at the same time possessed of all the charms of intellectual culture, breadth of outlook, ceaseless mobility and elasticity of mind.

' "It would be best to spend the first six months in a West-phalian peasant family – Roman Catholic unbrokenly for a thousand years; and the second six months, equally exclusively, among the medical students of Berlin, full of the flux of our day. When you have finished these two six months' immersions, ask yourself sincerely whether either group possessed that deep mysterious thing, the secret, the wisdom of life – which group knew, operatively, the meaning of birth, of suffering, of passion, of sin, of joy, of death. When you have done this I should like you to come and report the upshot to me."

'The American carried out this program,' Dr Martineau went on, 'and quite recently came and reported his conclusions to me. He had lived long enough with each group to have lived through a birth, a death, a grave moral lapse – troubles, sufferings, and successes of various kinds. The Catholic peasant group had been rough and clumsy, narrow in its sympathies, full of prejudices, and quite incapable of conceiving a modern doubt or difficulty. They were always treading on his corns.

'The sceptical medical group had been polished and supple, open to anything provided it were new or spelt revolt. These men were always anticipating all his tastes and fancies; and as regards religious practices or scruples, they had, of course, simply none.

'And yet, and yet! When face to face with the grim realities of life and death, those clumsy, superstitious, narrow popish peasants possessed a depth of insight, an assurance of action, an at-homeness of conviction, magnificent and massive, which was entirely lacking in the Berliners. When face to face with the same realities, the nimble, enlightened, materialist students were utterly helpless, without insight, action, conviction of any kind. The contrast was clear and decisive. Dr

Martineau ended by telling him that he must now return to America and work out for himself the implications of this startling experience.'

Here is another oblique comment to set beside that story. I was in France during the Easter vacation and was told of a well-known priest of a generation ago, who was also a well-known man of letters, one of the 'Immortals' in fact. Another priest said to him one day with obvious concern, 'I fear there are two men in me,' to which he replied, 'Oh! but there are twelve men in me.' What did he mean? I am not sure, but I suppose he meant the believer and the doubter, the artist and the scientist, the mystic and the rationalist, the conformist and the nonconformist, the lover of society and the lover of solitude, and so on.

Do you think that it is a bad thing to be more than one man? No doubt, in the extreme case it is, like the man in the Gospel who said his name was 'Legion': that was pathological. But, short of that, I wonder whether we should desire to be unified, quite at harmony in ourselves, rounded, consistent, our minds made up, so that everyone knows just where we stand. I allow that in the end a man needs to be one, unified, just as mankind does. But *in the end*. Is this what the theologians, with their inelegant jargon, call an eschatological possibility or promise?

But on the way to the end it may be better to be more than one man, pulled this way and that, with plenty of discords and jagged edges, trailing uncertainties, with clashing loyalties, ever and again amazed and perplexed and tongue-tied. Perhaps again this is why theologians have had so much to say about being justified by *faith*, for faith, unlike sight, stammers and is dumb.

It is because they were, each of them, at least two men that Balfour is the most interesting Prime Minister of this century and Lang the most interesting Archbishop of Canterbury. Can it be that all these churches and chapels and priests and religious activities, which still abound in Cambridge and *prima facie* seem to be a queer archaism, a hang-over from the past, are really here to prevent us from prematurely becoming one man and to keep us open to what is always beyond?

The Vicar said in his terminal letter that I should be giving you a last word. But I do not consider myself to be ripe for the utterance of any last words. If ever I were to utter a last word for public consumption, it would be something like what Père Lacordaire said: 'I hope to live and die a penitent Catholic, and an impenitent liberal.' However, I would rather break off than utter a last word. 'In divinity many things must be left abrupt,' as Francis Bacon said, and as St Mark knew when he ended his Gospel where he did.

CHAPTER XI

Theological Midwifery

━━

Well-intentioned but ill-informed people have often described me as a theologian, but I have deprecated the description. No doubt it depends on how strictly or how loosely one uses the term 'theologian'. If theology is taken to mean, in the words of the Oxford English Dictionary, 'the study or science which treats of God, his nature and attributes, and his relations with man and the universe' and a theologian to be one who is an expert in that study or science, I can lay no claim to the title, though as a priest I have naturally had an interest in the subject and have made some lowly incursions into it. On the other hand, if the meaning of theology is extended to include disciplines that are associated with it such as the study of ecclesiastical history, then I must allow that such expertise as I have acquired has been in that direction.

However, the point I want to make is that my métier has been much more that of a producer or editor of other people's theological compositions than that of a practitioner of the art myself. I have a precedent for speaking of midwifery in a literary context, for in the seventeenth century Francis Osborne, the friend of Thomas Hobbes, once said with reference to his publisher: 'There is another piece of mine ready to peep abroad, but that Mr Wood, my Midwife, is so taken up with raising an estate in Ireland, as he cannot attend the press.'

During my twenty-five years as editor of the journal *Theology* I was occupied in acting as a midwife to theologians and during that time I enabled a continuous succession of their pieces to 'peep abroad'. Many more articles and letters were always submitted to me than I could possibly bring to birth, but it was also my business to commission some special contributions. For example, I and my advisers gave a good deal of thought to series of articles by different authors that we wanted to publish. There were series on 'Great Preachers' and on 'Great Pastors', and another on 'Traditional Virtues re-assessed' which subsequently came out in book form; we also planned a series of 'Revised Reviews', that is, reappraisals of theological works that had made a mark when they first appeared but had ceased to be much read. I remember being surprised, when I asked G. L. Prestige, Gore's biographer, to do a revised review of *Lux Mundi*, by his telling me that he had not hitherto read the volume.

Again, my editing of the *Christian News-Letter* books during the Second World War (see p. 120) was an exercise in theological midwifery of a more popular kind. During that war I was also responsible together with F. L. Cross, who had a large practice in theological midwifery – witness his editing of *The Oxford Dictionary of the Christian Church* – for starting a 'Theological Literature Association'. We acted as its secretaries; Dr John Lowe, Dean of Christ Church, was the Chairman; Professor C. H. Dodd was the Vice-Chairman; and we had the support of a large number of authors. Our stated aims were:

(i) to find out what books were needed and what attempts were being made by individuals or organized bodies to meet the needs, (ii) to suggest to possible writers books that they should undertake, (iii) to bring together groups of writers who might be responsible for concerted literary work, and (iv) to draw up book-lists for the information of Christian apologists, students, etc.

Considerable interest was at first generated in the project and I have a large file of correspondence about various inquiries and proposals that we set in motion. However, after the war, when publishing conditions became more normal and publishers were themselves able to do what we had been attempting, the need for the association diminished and it was eventually wound up.

When I returned to Cambridge in 1956 I had not anticipated that any fresh engagements in theological midwifery awaited me, but in fact what I suppose was my most important undertaking of this kind soon began to take shape. It started like this. Some of the younger theologians in the university asked whether I was willing to convene and meet with them with a view to discussing their dissatisfaction with the state of English, or at least of Anglican, theological thought and to consider what might be done about it. The proposal was first broached to me by Howard Root, then Dean of Emmanuel College, now Professor of Theology at Southampton University.

The centenary was approaching of the publication of *Essays and Reviews,* a volume that had been produced by a group of Victorian divines (Frederick Temple, Benjamin Jowett, Mark Pattison, and others) in order to disturb what had seemed to them the ostrich-like condition of the English schools of theology in their time. Jowett had explained their purpose in these words: 'We are determined not to submit to this abominable system of terrorism, which prevents the statement of the plainest facts, and makes true theology or theological education impossible.' In 1957 it was not a system of terrorism that had to be countered but a state of complacency.

I must supply a brief account of the background of our enterprise: I say *our,* since I was in close sympathy with those who had invited me to confer with them. I have explained above (see chapter VIII) how I was affected by the change in the theological climate that took place in the 1930s and 1940s. I still think that what has been variously called 'neo-orthodoxy', 'biblical theology', 'the theology of crisis', had a salutary and bracing effect on those who were influenced by it and that it brought a wholesome sense of urgency and of desperate seriousness into our pulpits and even into some of our lecture-rooms.

But by the 1950s the enthusiasm that had been engendered by what some described as post-liberal or as post-critical kinds of theologizing was on the wane. Moreover, it had become evident that neo-orthodoxy, or whatever it should be called, had an obverse side. While it had undoubtedly been a shot in the arm for theologians and for theological students and given them a fresh zest for their subject, it had at the same time, and perhaps for that reason, led to their cultivating a language and, one might say, a jargon that prevented them from being able to communicate with interested people outside their enclave. This is a fatal condition for theology to get into, since by definition what it is supposed to be talking about is a matter of concern for all men. It must no doubt have its specialists but it must never become a mere specialism. When theologians are on speaking terms only with themselves they are doomed to frustration and indeed to damnation.

Another drawback that had become apparent by the 1950s was that in theological circles it seemed to be generally assumed that the foundations of belief were secure and one could happily let oneself become absorbed in questions of superstructure or in the corollaries of belief. I had found, for instance, as editor of *Theology*, that the topics that appealed to the pundits were such things as episcopacy and baptism and schemes for Church union, whereas the reality of God and belief in Christ as the final revelation of God were treated as axiomatic. What used to be known as 'natural theology' was neglected except by some Gifford lecturers, and philosophical theology was at a discount. It seemed to be thought that the authority of the Bible could be taken for granted. Earlier in the century the liberal Protestants and the Catholic modernists had been concerned with these fundamental questions and not with what was peripheral. They might have proposed wrong or inadequate answers to the fundamental questions, but the questions were still there and needed to be taken up again.

It was considerations like these that led us to believe that some new lead was called for or at least a *cri de coeur*. But we did not rush into action – or into publication. What we did was to constitute a quite unofficial group of about a dozen members of the divinity faculty at Cambridge who shared the concerns that I have just sought to indicate. We fortunately had some cool-headed seniors like John Burnaby and George Woods as well as those who could be fittingly described as younger theologians. We met periodically in my rooms at King's and each of us in turn submitted essays about that aspect of the theological task that was most on our minds. These essays were frankly and critically discussed and subsequently revised and re-discussed. Though we were all good friends and not over-solemn about what we were doing, there was naturally a bit of tension at times. For example, I had some difficulty in keeping George Woods and Harry Williams in double harness: both of them were essential members of the group.

At one stage we spent a long weekend together at Launde Abbey in Leicestershire. By that time we had decided that we had sufficient well-sifted material and sufficient coherence to warrant us in producing a volume of essays which we hoped would serve as something of a manifesto. This was the origin of the volume entitled *Soundings: essays concerning Christian understanding*. I think I suggested the title and also discovered our text from a seventeenth-century bishop of Gloucester: 'Man hath but a shallow sound and a short reach, and dealeth onely by probabilities and likely-hoods.' Our standpoint was stated in the opening paragraph of my editorial introduction:

> The authors of this volume of essays cannot persuade themselves that the time is ripe for major works of theological construction or reconstruction. It is a time for ploughing, not reaping; or, to use the metaphor we have chosen for our title, it is a time for making soundings, not charts or maps. If this be so, we do not have to apologize for our inability to do what we hope will be possible in a future generation. We can best serve the cause of truth and of the

Church by candidly confessing where our perplexities lie, and not by making claims which, so far as we can see, theologians are not at present in a position to justify.

The book became well-known and does not call for further description here. It was published by the Cambridge University Press, of which I was at the time a syndic; it had a much larger circulation and received much more attention than we could have anticipated. In part this may have been because it became caught up in, or associated with, a number of other unforeseen and quite independent initiatives that made their appearance about the same time. I will just mention some of these in which I was not involved, before coming to one in which I was involved.

Dr John Robinson's *Honest to God* was the most conspicuous apparition. It had phenomenal sales, partly because he had recently become a bishop, an adventitious circumstance that was well advertised. Although he had been a don at Cambridge when we formed the *Soundings* group, we had deliberately not invited him to join it, because he seemed then to be still an apostle of biblical theology and of the liturgical movement. He wrote *Honest to God* after he left Cambridge and we knew nothing about it till it was in print.

Another small book, *God is no more* (1963) by Werner and Lotte Pelz, with a foreword by Edward Carpenter, was also of quite independent origin. It was more radical and better written than *Honest to God* and made quite an impact at the time, though it is now forgotten. The same may be said of Ronald Gregor Smith's *The New Man: Christianity and Man's Coming of Age*, which had been published in 1956: he was an old friend of mine, but the line of thought he was developing in Scotland had nothing to do with our English initiatives.

It was also about this time that Teilhard de Chardin's posthumous publications began to appear in English translations, and were regarded as opening up a new and exciting style of theological thinking. It did not particularly appeal to me, though I was for a time a member of the Teilhard de Chardin Association: that was because I had been unable to resist the seductive charms of its honorary secretary, Mrs Croose Parry! (I remember allowing her to speak for longer than I ought to have done when I was presiding over a conference of the University Teachers Group at Oxford.) I have always had a prejudice against theologians who have refrained from publishing what they have believed to be true out of deference or obedience to ecclesiastical authority: I held this against Teilhard.

Much more important was the explosion of fresh theological work in the Roman Catholic Church that was set off by the pontificate of Pope John XXIII and the Second Vatican Council. Evidently, there were numerous groups and individuals, including cardinals and bishops, who had been waiting for a moment of release from the restrictions that had been imposed for generations by the Roman Curia.

Back in England, there were other independent initiatives at this time in the field of Christian ethics, such as *Towards a Quaker View of Sex* (1963) and *Christian Personal Values and Sexual Morality* by Douglas Rhymes (1964). Mr Rhymes was a canon of Southwark Cathedral where one of his colleagues, when he was appointed, protested against being required to assent to the Thirty-Nine Articles, though the sting of his protest was drawn by his assenting to them all the same. This was the diocese in which John Robinson held office as Bishop of Woolwich, and a consequence was that people started talking about Southbank religion or Southbank morality, either approvingly or disapprovingly according to their prepossessions.

I had nothing to do with these independent manifestations of theological unconventionality in the early 1960s, and indeed disapproved of some of them. Nor did I think much of the so-called 'death of God' theology or of the 'secular Christianity' that were for a time propagated in the later 1960s, chiefly in the USA. I said what little I thought of them in a chapter on 'A Decade of Fermentation' that I added to a new edition of my book, *The Church in an Age of Revolution*.

But I must now deal with the other independent initiative in which I was involved. This was a course of four open lectures for members of the university that was projected for the Lent term 1963 by the Cambridge divinity faculty on 'Fundamental Objections to Christianity'. There were four lecturers: D. M. MacKinnon on 'Moral Objections'; H. A. Williams on 'Psychological Objections'; myself on 'Historical Objections'; and J. S. Bezzant on 'Intellectual Objections'. The lectures drew a very large attendance of about fifteen hundred each week, and were followed up by discussion groups in many of the colleges. An enterprising publisher undertook to bring the lectures out as a book with remarkable speed, and it became something of a publishing success: it was included for several weeks in the top ten of best-selling books. It was also translated into several foreign languages. I had acted as editor and so count it as one of my exercises in theological midwifery. In my introduction to the book I said:

> The aim of the lectures . . . was not to provide answers to objections to Christian belief. There is a spate of books which set out to do that. We hold that it is more important to try to plumb the depths of the objections, without complacently assuming that answers are readily available. Above all in a university, Christians must seek to understand the fundamental doubts to which their faith is exposed in this age of the world.

I do not myself rate this book highly. Nothing like so much concerted work went into it as into *Soundings*. But I think the lectures themselves served their purpose so far as Cambridge was concerned. The effect of their publication is much more difficult to assess. Reviewers were sharply divided on the matter. The reviewer in *The Listener* (27 June 1963) said: 'In effect it is like seeing the resident firemen of Christianity acting as incendiaries, cutting their own hoses, in order to demonstrate how well they understand the human condition of arson.' On the other hand, William Barclay in *The Expository Times* (June 1963) concluded: 'This is an intensely important book. Any thinking Christian who reads it will be better able to face himself, the world, and God.' I consider that this was too favourable a verdict. I am happier with what Ronald Gregor Smith wrote in the *Glasgow Herald* (22 May 1963):

> Their general aim is to see the modern objections to Christian belief with as much honesty as possible, and in doing this to set the right tone for intelligent acceptance or refusal of that belief. One thing they have in common: they do not attempt what Reinhold Niebuhr once said of theological students, that when they were faced with intractable problems they straightaway took an elevator for the eternal.

The effect of our Cambridge publications in conjunction with the other essays in so-called radical thought that I have mentioned above was to make theology for some years an unwontedly popular subject in all sorts of circles, and credit or discredit was showered upon Cambridge as the centre of the fermentation. The media too displayed an interest in what they called 'Cambridge theology' or 'the new theology'. I refused to adopt this manner of speaking: on the one hand, there were many theologians in Cambridge who were not implicated in either *Soundings* or *Objections to Christianity* and may well have been embarrassed by them, and on the other hand it was entirely misleading to suggest that anything like a new theological synthesis or system had been propounded or even adumbrated.

Nevertheless, the idea got around that something was happening at Cambridge which was worth knowing about. We had many theologically interested visitors from abroad. For some years I was myself constantly invited to speak in different parts of Britain on some such subject as 'Ferment in theology'. I did so in many places and certainly found a much livelier interest had been aroused in theology than I had experienced for a long time. I also engaged in a number of discussions on the radio and television. Some of my remarks about the Church and the clergy in one of them caused quite a storm, and for several weeks in November 1962 I was abused in *The Church Times* under the banner headline: DR VIDLER'S ATTACK ON THE CHURCH. That gave me no sleepless nights, and anyhow I also received much appreciative correspondence.

I have never sought access to the media but my opinion was – and is – that if one is asked to discuss what one has said in print, it is a duty to do so and a duty to speak as frankly and honestly as possible. The hazard must be faced that many listeners or viewers are likely to misunderstand what is said and to be mystified or scandalized.

As regards the general outcome of all this agitation in the usually placid waters of theological reflection and speculation, in which my midwifery had played a modest part, I agree with what David Edwards said of it in his book *The Honest to God Debate:*

> What has been achieved so far has been little more than a series of gestures to show that some Christians are anxious to enter into a real conversation with more typical citizens of our secular society. What is needed is not a premature theological synthesis, and even more certainly not the organization of a new religious party, but a host of other experiments in thought and life (p. 24).

I had more to say about this and about the history of theological thought in this century in my Robertson lectures, *Twentieth Century Defenders of the Faith,* where I ended by saying:

> I am glad that there are the beginnings of a promising commotion in the churches, and that windows and sluices are being opened which twenty years ago seemed to be pretty

firmly closed. I find it encouraging that, though there have naturally been expressions of alarm, churches do not at present seem to be trying to suppress their radicals.

I should perhaps add that I have acted as midwife to the departed as well as to the living. In 1958 I introduced and edited a new edition of F. D. Maurice's *The Kingdom of Christ* which had been out of print for a long time. The new edition was significant of the revived interest in Maurice as a theologian. In 1959 I introduced and edited a book of John Middleton Murry's 'lay sermons'. They were addresses that he had given on Sunday evenings to his farming community in Norfolk. I called the book *Not as the Scribes,* which I regarded as a well-chosen title. In 1963 I introduced and edited a new edition of George Tyrrell's *Christianity at the Cross Roads.* Of all the theologians I have written about, Tyrrell has meant more to me than any of the others and I return to him most often, perhaps because his theology was inchoate as all theology ought to be. As he said, 'surely the babe just born knows as much of the world and its ways as the wisest of us can know of the ways of God, whose sway stretches over heaven and earth, time and eternity.'

CHAPTER XII

Return to Rye

When I returned to Rye in August 1967 the ancient part of the town had not much changed since I had come to know it intimately in my youth. A few fine old houses had regrettably been replaced by modern shops, and bombs during the Second World War had destroyed Henry James's garden room in which he wrote his novels, the early-nineteenth-century Methodist church, and the pleasant offices on the strand of our family business which had since been wound up. A bomb had also done good work in shattering an unsightly stained-glass east window in the parish church. It had been replaced by a comparatively worthy one, and there were two other fine new windows (one of the Benedicite) that had been given between the wars by E. F. Benson.

Many houses that had been covered with stucco in the eighteenth or nineteenth century had been restored to their original appearance, and I should say that on the whole Rye was now an even more beautiful place in which to live than it had been before. The Friars of the Sack, which is the oldest house in the town, had not changed externally, but since I inherited it I had done much to improve its internal commodiousness.

In another respect Rye had changed considerably. The old town on its hill, sometimes now known as 'the citadel', was by this time more or less surrounded by modern houses, in some cases lamentable stretches of ribbon development but more recently by quite tolerable housing estates. A strange consequence of this is that, although Rye now embraces a much

Winchelsea and the Brede Valley from Rye

larger built-up area than it did previously, its population has hardly increased at all. This is to be accounted for by the facts that there are fewer children and more elderly retired folk, that houses are more sparsely occupied, and that quite a proportion of them are second or weekend houses.

In 1967 Rye was still a borough, as it had been since 1289, and was managing its own affairs, but the Rye Rural District Council, which used to be responsible for the surrounding villages, had been absorbed in the Battle Rural District Council, an omen of graver absorptions to come.

I was fortunate in being able to return not only to my native town but to the house in which I had been born. You will not easily find people of my age who are living in the house in which they were born. I am still often asked whether I do not greatly miss Cambridge, but I answer no, except for my friends there and the university library. I should add the singing of King's College choir, were it not that I have about fifty of its records to which I constantly listen. As regards my friends, one advantage of living in a beautiful place of historic interest is that they welcome an opportunity of visiting it even if they are not eager to see me! I have lots of visitors, especially in the summer months. Although there can be no substitute for having a university library within five minutes' walk, still in the course of my life I have built up a large working library, for which I have room in my house at Rye, and in a study in the garden, which my father had constructed out of an army hut after the First World War. I am also able to make periodical use of the university library at Cambridge and of other libraries.

I have noticed that many people, not least clergymen, after they have retired, are fond of remarking with complacency, and even with pride, that they have been busier since they retired than ever they were before. I had no intention myself of being tempted to make so incongruous a remark. I took two preventive measures. Whereas in my cottage at Shepreth I had been able to dispense altogether with the telephone and so to include in my letter heading 'No telephone, *D.G.*', I did allow myself to possess the noxious instrument at Rye but made sure that my number was ex-directory. I have given it only to a few close friends, and then on the strict condition that they will never communicate it to anyone else. This precaution has saved me not only from being bounced into making unconsidered engagements, but also from being rung up on Saturday evenings by vicars' wives, asking me to take their husband's duty on the morrow as he has an incipient cold. I could adopt this attitude with an easy conscience since there is at present no shortage of clergy in and around Rye, and in any case I believe in congregations' doing it themselves when for any reason a priest is not available.

The other preventive measure I took was to make a rule that I would not accept more than one engagement a month that involved my being away from home for a night. This has been very salutary and has prevented me from gadding about all over the place and never continuing in one stay, though it has also required me to refuse some alluring invitations.

I am not however saying that I have been unoccupied or

indolent since I retired. For one thing, except for the services of a good lady who comes in to clean for four hours a week, I entirely look after myself and my house and garden: I bake my own bread and do my own cooking and guests tell me that my efforts are not discreditable. I have continued to do quite a lot of book reviewing and examining academic theses. I have been able to accept invitations to lecture or speak in universities in France and the USA as well as in many parts of Britain, and I have been easy-going with local invitations that do not entail being away from Rye for a night. In 1975 I spent a fortnight in the Seychelles where the Bishop, George Briggs, an old friend and fellow member of the Oratory of the Good Shepherd, asked me to do a variety of interesting things.

But what has chiefly prevented me from being idle has been involvement in local affairs, both in municipal government and in the work of a number of voluntary societies. I had not anticipated this involvement. For nearly fifty years I had been no more than an occasional visitor to Rye and expected on my return to live an obscure and secluded life, renewing my acquaintance with those friends of my youth who still survived and making some new ones but not cutting a public figure of any sort, unless it were as an intermittent preacher.

However, within about six months of my return I was asked by the local branch of the ratepayers' association whether I would be a candidate for election to the borough council. The Rye Borough Council had sixteen members all of whom were professedly 'independent', that is, they did not represent political parties. The ratepayers' association was a kind of ginger group in the town that was trying to enliven local government and to inject some fresh blood into the borough council. I agreed to stand at the next municipal election in May 1968, and thanks to the support of the ratepayers' association and thanks also, no doubt, to the facts that my family name had been well-known in Rye for well over a century and that I was myself a Ryer born and bred, I was elected at the top of the poll with what was said to be the largest number of votes that any candidate had ever received.

During the following three years I took an active part in the work of the council, attending committee meetings and speaking often at council meetings. I became keenly interested in the needs of our local community and in the mechanics of local government. I observed that the psychology of municipal bodies is very similar to that of the ecclesiastical and academic bodies with which I was already familiar, though naturally the members of the Rye Borough Council, even if they had more horse sense than the fellows of King's, had a lower I.Q. It was difficult to get any good, rational or relevant argumentation going at our council meetings. All committee meetings tend to become boring if the chairmanship is of poor quality and if there are one or two members who talk too much. Much patience is required by those who give time to public service. Speaking of committee meetings and the recent ambition of students to become members of academic bodies, I could not agree more with what Christopher Hollis has said:

> In all the world there is surely no duller task than that of the administration of an educational body and that anyone should demand as a right and privilege to sit on these committees is unbelievable and surely in itself proof of an adolescent lack of maturity.

It was during this period that the proposals for the re-organization of local government were being pressed upon us. I made a careful study of the Maud Report. I could see that where a small municipality like Rye was concerned the case for some reform was unanswerable. It was obvious that some of our services, such as refuse collection, could be more economically and efficiently managed by a larger unit of local government. I favoured the unitary proposals of the Maud Report which, I believed, would lead to the county council's dealing with what could be best managed by a more widespread organization, while Rye itself would be left to manage the rest of its affairs as heretofore. I regret to say that a majority of the members of our borough council voted instead for a two-tier system, with its doubling of bureaucracy and staffs with large salaries, such as the Conservative government eventually adopted and which has had melancholy results for Rye as indeed for many other places too.

If there had to be a two-tier system with county and district councils, the obvious place with which Rye should have been linked is Hastings, which is our natural centre, and that is what both Hastings and Rye wanted. Instead it was decreed that, in spite of local desires, Rye should become part of an unwieldy area known as Rother, which covered Bexhill and the former Battle rural district. While Rye has ample and direct communications with Hastings, it has no direct communications with either Bexhill or Battle.

My three-year term as a councillor ended at the beginning of May 1971. I did not stand for re-election since I thought I should make way for younger candidates. On 19 April I wrote in my journal: '5.30 p.m. – 6.30 p.m. council meeting: the last I shall attend as a councillor. I spoke for Rye going in with Hastings under local government reform.' When I said it was the last meeting that I should attend 'as a councillor', it was an accurate prediction, though it was by no means the last council meeting that I should attend. Before I go on with the unforeseen tale of my further participation in municipal government, I must turn to things that had been happening meanwhile.

One of the greatest pleasures that attended my return to Rye was that I became a near neighbour of Malcolm Muggeridge, for Robertsbridge where he had now settled is only about ten miles from Rye. We have thus been able to meet about twice a week in order to walk and talk and engage in various diversions. If, when one retires, it is a great boon to be able to live again in the house in which one was born, it is a still greater boon to be within easy reach of one's oldest and closest friend.

Among our diversions bee-keeping has a place. I introduced the Muggeridges to this and, although they like honey more than they do the manipulation of bees, an apiary is now a firmly established feature of their garden. Another of our diversions, if it may be so called, is a bible study group for about fifteen people which meets weekly for certain periods of the year either in my house or in theirs. We begin with a record of sacred music, then it falls to me to expound or comment on whatever book in the Scriptures we are studying, and this is followed by discussion, and finally by convivial talk over a cup of tea. Sometimes we have enjoyed being shown some of the splendid films that Malcolm has done for television (a mechanism which neither he nor I possess but which can be laid on for special occasions). Each Christmas we have a carol service in the crypt of the ancient Cistercian abbey at Salehurst which is quite near the Muggeridges' home and where, so far as we know, there had been no act of worship since the dissolution of the monasteries.

But our principal joint diversion at this time was the making of the television film about St Paul in which we took part together in the spring of 1970. This attracted some publicity. I need say little about it since we have told the story of the making of the film and how we were affected by it in our book *Paul, Envoy Extraordinary* (1972). It was for me an intensely interesting and instructive experience, although at the time it was very fatiguing and I was glad to get home.

During the summer that followed our exploits in the Near East the Muggeridges rented a farm house in southern Ireland near Clonakilty: I spent about a month with them and lost my heart to their engaging Canadian grandsons who were there, too, with their parents. In the mornings Malcolm and I worked. There was the published version of our film to be prepared, though most of the work on the scripts was done later. I was considering a proposal that I should edit a new edition of Newman's *Idea of a University* but that did not come to anything. We made a number of expeditions on one of which we discovered the cottage where Michael Collins was born, and on another the spot where he was murdered. The Canadian Muggeridges are Roman Catholics and in the evenings we used to study the Epistle to the Romans, but there is no necessary connection between those two statements! While in Ireland I took the opportunity of letting my beard grow much longer than it had been heretofore, but my hope that it might rival St Jerome's in length has been disappointed. I was however greeted as Karl Marx when I went to lecture at Strasbourg university, at a time when the theological students there were on strike. On previous occasions my beard had led to my being hailed only as Haile Selassie, Dr Joad or Bernard Shaw. Nowadays, whenever I meet small children for the first time I announce that I am Father Christmas to save them from the impertinence of addressing me by that title.

Later in 1970 I thought I was becoming decrepit, as I had aches and pains in various parts of my body. I consulted more than one medical adviser and tried various kinds of treatment, including acupuncture, but to no avail. In the following year, supposing that I was likely to become increasingly inactive or sedentary, I went for a week's residential course near Canterbury for beginners in painting. I was much taken with it and was intending to make painting in oils my main hobby, when I was told about the medicinal virtues of cider vinegar. I began to take a daily dose (as I have continued to do ever since): my aches and pains were quickly cured and I was able to resume all my previous interests and activities. My potential proclivity for painting has since then been kept in reserve.

It was on 25 January 1972 that a member of the Rye Borough Council surprised me by asking whether he might propose me for the office of Mayor during the coming year. I said that I could consider it only if I was assured that it was the wish of a majority of members of the council. The outcome was that I was unanimously elected on 6 March to serve from the follow-

ing May. My chief feeling at the moment was of the pleasure that
my father would have derived from my following in his foot-
steps and in those of his father and grandfather and of other
members of our family. Later on, when I was interviewed for
the French radio, I started to explain about my ancestors'
having been mayors before me. I began 'Mon père, mon
grandpère, et mon . . .' but could not think what 'great-
grandfather' is in French, and so had to be prompted. We
do not often speak of our great-grandparents even in our own
language. My election was all the more gratifying in that I
was not a member of the council. This, though legally in order,
was very unusual. So far as I know, the only previous mayor of
Rye who had not been a member of the council was E. F.
Benson, who had also been a King's man.

The duties of a mayor of Rye were not so exacting as those of
the mayor of a larger borough, but they were sufficiently
demanding to make me eschew, so far as possible, other
engagements during my period of office which lasted from May
1972 to the end of March 1974, since I was invited to serve
for a second year and so became the last mayor of the Borough
of Rye. Under local government reorganization, which took
effect from 1 April 1974, we lost our status as a borough and
could have only what is known as a 'town mayor'.

As mayor I had much to learn about what was expected of me.
I was fortunate in having the guidance of an experienced
town clerk, secretary and town sergeant: the last could serve as
my chauffeur in case of need, but, needless to say, I was not
provided with one of those large official motor cars that more
affluent boroughs could afford. Being wifeless, I was free to
select my mayoress and was happy that my cousin and near
neighbour, Mrs John Vidler, was willing to undertake that office.
It had been a cause of great sadness to me that John Vidler,
the well-known reforming prison governor, had died shortly
after I returned to Rye. His father had been Mayor of Rye in
his time. I could also select the mayor's chaplain. During my

first year I was supported in this way by the Rye Methodist minister, who was then moved elsewhere. I had hoped to have our Roman Catholic priest for my second year but he too was moved away from Rye by the authorities of his church at this juncture, and so I turned instead to the assistant curate of the parish church.

It was my practice to visit our council offices each day in order to attend to correspondence and other business. In Rye it was the tradition that the mayor not only presided at meetings of the council but also attended the meetings of all committees of the council, some of which were of inordinate duration! But most of my time was taken up with banquets, ceremonies and social occasions of one kind or another, all of which I thoroughly enjoyed, except for the intolerable noise made by dance bands. My mayoress was no more eager to dance than I was, so when the time came for that we used to go home. I became accustomed to, if not adept at, presenting prizes, crowning beauty queens, and making speeches of all sorts.

My engagements were by no means confined to Rye and its immediate neighbourhood. Other Sussex mayors were generous in inviting all mayors and mayoresses in the county to their principal functions and Sussex, it should be remembered, extends as far as Chichester in the west. Then, since Rye is a member of the Confederation of the Cinque Ports, its mayor takes part in all the functions of that body, which during my term of office included an exchange of visits at Dover with the officers of HMS *Albion* (a ship adopted by the Cinque Ports), a Venetian carnival on the Royal Military Canal at Hythe, and the installation of a new Constable of Dover Castle. A consequence of all these excursions in Sussex and Kent was that we made many new friends whom we were pleased to meet again and again whenever there was an assembly of municipal dignitaries.

On my two mayoring days my health was proposed by two of the best after-dinner speakers in the country, by Malcolm

Muggeridge in 1972 and by Lord Redcliffe-Maud in 1973, and on the last day of Rye's existence as a borough (31 March 1974) Malcolm was also the preacher at a special service in the parish church. Moreover he was good enough to present to the town hall a bronze bust of my unworthy self, sculptured by Betty Miller. It now stands in the mayor's parlour.

When I ceased to be mayor and involved in local government, I continued to take part in local affairs. I was the first chairman of the Rye Preservation Society which already has much good work to its credit. I am chairman of the Rye Museum of which my father had been the founder and first curator, and which in 1975 received the National Heritage award for the museum of the year in the south-east of England. This was the result of the devoted work of the present curator, Mr G. S. Bagley, and of his team of helpers. I am also chairman of several other organizations in Rye which it would be tedious to specify. However, under my chairmanship they can be sure that their meetings will always start punctually and will not be unduly prolonged. I made one reappearance in the field of ecclesiastical administration when the Bishop of Chichester asked me to chair a commission that was to investigate and report on the whole subject of communications in the diocese: this exercise revealed to me many facts and possibilities of which I had previously been unaware.

My regular way of entertaining my friends in Rye has been to have a monthly 'at home' at tea time on the same day in every month. This was to revive a practice that I recall when I was young and that apparently died out during the First World War. I came across an old visiting card of my mother's on which the words 'First Fridays' were printed. Everyone then knew it meant that she was 'at home' for tea on the first Friday in every month. As soon as I get my engagement book for the next year I fill in my 'at homes' on the second Wednesday in every month. I much prefer this mode of entertaining to cock-tail parties at which one has to stand up all the time and is deafened by the babble of conversation.

I take the view that if one lives at Rye one does not need to go away for holidays and I have less and less inclination to do so. However, since I retired I have spent three holidays in France – one in Provence, another at Grenoble, and the third was a pilgrimage with John Collins to the tomb of our old friend Alfred Loisy. I have frequently revisited Cambridge, especially since 1972 when King's honoured me by electing me into an honorary fellowship. When Harold Nicolson was made an honorary fellow of Balliol he said that 'of all honours this earth can give' that was the one he most desired. Certainly there is no honour I have valued more than that which King's thus bestowed on me.

One of my diversions used to be writing occasional letters to *The Times* newspaper. My letters were usually quite short and, I am glad to say, were nearly always published. A few of them, I hope, may be recalled without boring my readers. When in 1965 it was announced that the Church of England was going to appoint another commission on the relations of Church and State (there had already been three within my own recollection) I wrote the following letter upon which, I remember, Lord Reith, who was a good judge of such letters, went out of his way to congratulate me:

> So there is to be yet another commission on the relations of Church and State, in spite of the competence of previous commissions and the inaction that followed the reception of their reports.
>
> Will anyone who is wise enough to be qualified to serve on the new commission be stupid enough to accept an invitation to do so? (13 November 1965)

I took a malicious pleasure in sticking pins into archbishops. Thus for example:

> The Archbishop of York, when addressing Convocation, is reported to have deplored 'witty asides' about the Church

when churchmen are speaking in public. I had not noticed them. I expect, if you had been able to publish a full report of his speech, it would have appeared that he said something even more severe about pious platitudes, humbug and bores. (22 January 1965)

When after Dr Fisher's retirement I claimed to set him a good example in a certain matter I received many felicitations from bishops and others who had been much tried by his persistent interventions in business that was no longer his:

> In one respect, though in only one, I can claim to set a good example to Archbishop Lord Fisher. When I retired, I determined to refrain from intervening, or seeking to exert an influence, in my previous fields of responsibility. It is in fact delightful to be detached from them and to cultivate other interests. I happen to know that many of the Archbishop's friends and admirers . . . would be much relieved if he would follow my example in this single, but not unimportant, respect. (12 June 1969)

One or two of my interventions in more mundane correspondences may not have been without effect. Soon after I wrote the following letter, airlines began to have special compartments for non-smokers:

> The problems that beset non-smokers in trains are trivial in comparison with those that beset non-smokers in flying machines. I have had to do a lot of flying during the past twelve months, but I am thankful to say that I have now been given grace to vow that I will not fly again until non-smokers are accommodated. This could be done in either of two ways which there is no need to specify. (30 November 1970)

In 1962 there was an engaging correspondence about 'reading in bed', to which I made this contribution:

> Shetland shawls be hanged! Shawls are of course invaluable

when one is up and about. But for reading in bed what is needed is a specially knitted woollen cape which fastens at the neck with one large button. This keeps its position better than a shawl and is more comfortably discarded than a sweater or a dressing-gown when the moment comes for sleep. Then again one of the many advantages of night-shirts over the now obsolescent pyjamas is that they button at the wrists. (5 January 1962)

But much the best letter in this correspondence was one from Mr O. W. H. Cooke of Uxbridge:

A fig for dressing up! The sole requirement is a literate wife with a melodious voice. (8 January 1962)

When the Young Liberals threatened to take direct action against juggernauts, I was able to let off steam on a subject about which I felt and feel very strongly:

May an Old Non-Liberal say how strongly he approves of the action that the Young Liberals intend to take with regard to juggernauts? People who suppose that mere talk or voting will nerve our legislators to stand up to the road haulage interests are living in a fool's paradise. Something much more drastic and provocative needs to be done.

As for the notion that the remedy for juggernauts is to build more motorways, that would mean playing more havoc with the countryside and with valuable agricultural land just when there is the happy prospect that all oil-fed traffic will have to grind to a halt in the foreseeable future. Meanwhile juggernauts should be banned in Britain. (29 August 1973)

But my last and longest letter to *The Times* had the biggest follow-up. It was headed 'An Awkward Shortage':

I shall be grateful if you will allow me to draw public attention to the hardship that is increasingly experienced by septuagenarian men when they are away from home, and *a fortiori* by octogenarians and nonagenarians. I refer to the disappearance of the chamber pot as an article of bedroom furniture, or rather of guest room furniture. Of course some bedrooms have a bathroom directly attached to them and in that case I make no complaint. But, like many of my contemporaries, I am often invited to spend the night in a room that has no such convenience. We do not like to disturb our hosts by wandering about dark passages in quest of light switches and uncertain doors and at last by the noise of flushing.

We plead for the restoration of the traditional chamber pot to its rightful place either under the bed or in a bedside cabinet. It is true that most of them now seem to have found their way into antique shops and thence to the United States. But various sizes in plastic are obtainable and, for my part, I am ready to settle for one of these as a substitute for an elegant piece of china.

I would add that I entirely agree with the late Dick Sheppard that the recipients of such relief should always be responsible in the morning for emptying and cleansing any receptacle which they have used, and not leave that operation as a chore for their hostess or any minion of hers. (6 May 1976)

This was followed by over two dozen highly entertaining letters in *The Times* as well as by many more that were addressed to me personally. The letters in *The Times* were reproduced or commented on far and wide, especially in the USA and Canada. I myself sent a short, second letter to the paper, which I hoped would indirectly serve as an acknowledgement of the many that I had received but was not disposed to reply to at the present postal rates. But despite the advertisement that they had received through my initiative, those responsible refused to publish it and offered only lame excuses for not doing so. I therefore told them that they would be bothered with no further letters.

My return to Rye made it possible for me to have the company of domestic animals which had not been feasible when I had lived in college at King's. At Windsor I had had a dog, a corgi, which had been given to me by an amiable teacher whose work for the London Bachelor of Divinity I had supervised while I was still at Hawarden. I called him Zimri, since I was set on calling my animals by names in the Bible beginning with Z. Zimri's only fault was that, whenever I set out in his company from my house in Windsor Castle, he barked so loudly and so persistently that I could never conceal my movements. He could not accompany me to Cambridge and spent his last years in my housekeeper's genial care.

At Rye I took speedy steps to procure a puppy and a kitten. The puppy, a Jack Russell terrier, who had been named Donald by his breeder, I renamed Zadok. The trouble with him has been not an excessive disposition to bark but an incapacity to resist chasing rabbits and other people's cats. The kitten, with whom his relations soon became cordial, was given to me and I named her Zillah. When a clergyman is present at a party or meeting in my house, I often tell the company that he will be able to tell them where Zillah comes in the Bible but, alas! he never can, not even the present Archbishop of Canterbury to whom I put this testing question! Zadok and Zillah are small enough to occupy the same basket, and they excite the wonder of my guests by assiduously washing each other and by performing other antics. When I am away, Zadok frequently stays with the Muggeridges. They allege that he once killed one of their chickens, but in spite of that are more indulgent to him than I am and give him tit-bits that he never gets from me.

I do not know whether an autobiography ought to end with a *confessio fidei*. George Cockin, when he was Bishop of Bristol, used to tell me that he hoped after he retired to write a book in which he would lay bare his soul and say as frankly as possible what he believed and what he did not believe. I have done enough of that already. I have nothing of importance to

Zadok and Zillah

retract in my books such as *Christian Belief* (*see* p. 145) or *Windsor Sermons* (*see* p. 163) and the rest. When I retired, I judged that fifty years of reading theology had been enough (I distinguish Church history from theology), especially as it is not a subject in which there seem to be many more advances to be made. Furthermore, the work of contemporary theologians, with very few exceptions, does not impress or enlighten me as much as that of those whom I used to read. Thus I have no impulse to produce any more essays in theology myself, nor am I likely to be called upon again to act as a midwife.

I am not, however, a complacent or satisfied believer; nor have I ever been that. My difficulties or doubts arise more from imagination or lack of imagination than from reason. I have seen no reason to admit that any of the alternatives to Christianity have more to be said for them than Christianity itself. It seems to me extremely unreasonable and inhuman to believe, as I suppose secular humanists must do, that all that mankind has experienced and all its potentialities will be as though they had never been when life on this planet becomes extinct.

On the other hand, I am incapable of imagining what lies beyond this life and I regard Christian doctrines about the hereafter as no more than the first lispings of children. I see that in my journal I have from time to time confessed my agnosticism. On one occasion I acknowledged that I was 'an agnostic believer', on another 'a sceptic in faith's clothing'. Such confessions, I suppose, illustrate the ambivalence that must be experienced by many thoughtful believers today and by thoughtful unbelievers too. Nor is this state of affairs so novel as it may appear to be to those who are unacquainted with the confessions of past men and women of faith. George Herbert knew all about it when he wrote:

> Profaneness in my head,
> Defects and darknesse in my breast,
> A noise of passions ringing me for dead
> Unto a place where is no rest:
> Poor priest, thus am I drest.

> Onely another head
> I have, another heart and breast,
> Another musick, making live, not dead,
> Without whom I could have no rest:
> In him I am well drest.

Robert Leighton is another of my favourite authors of *le grand siècle* and I take comfort from his saying: 'Some travel on in a covert, cloudy day, and get home by it, have so much light as to know their way, and yet do not at all clearly see the bright and full sunshine of assurance; others have it breaking forth at times, and anon under a cloud; and some have it more constantly.'

Let me then say in conclusion that I believe with Father Tyrrell that God 'cares more that we should grip his hand in the dark than dream about his face', and that with him I hope that 'death is no breach of life, but the estuary where the river of time widens silently into the sea of eternity'. Or rather with Lamennais, using a different and a better metaphor, I would say: '*A mesure que j'approche du terme, je me sens plus attiré vers ce monde mystérieux dont celui-ci n'est que le portique ouvert à tous les vents, au soleil, à la pluie, comme si la Providence avait voulu nous inspirer l'envie d'entrer dans le temple.*'

Deo gratias.

INDEX

═══

206